When
FOOTBALL *Was*
FOOTBALL

ARSENAL

First published in 2009

A catalogue record for this book is available from the British Library

ISBN: 978-1-844259-47-2

Published by Haynes Publishing, Sparkford, Yeovil,
Somerset BA22 7JJ, UK
Tel: 01963 442030 Fax: 01963 440001
Int. tel: +44 1963 442030 Int. fax: +44 1963 440001
E-mail: sales@haynes.co.uk
Website: www.haynes.co.uk

Haynes North America Inc., 861 Lawrence Drive,
Newbury Park, California 91320, USA

All images © Mirrorpix

Creative Director: Kevin Gardner
Packaged for Haynes by Green Umbrella Publishing

Printed and bound in Britain by J F Print Ltd., Sparkford, Somerset

When FOOTBALL *Was* FOOTBALL

ARSENAL

A Nostalgic Look at a Century of the Club

Paul Joseph

Contents

Introduction

So comprehensively has Arsène Wenger rebranded Arsenal Football Club that it is possible to forget the 100-plus years of history that came before him.

Yet there remain curious parallels that glue together the club's past and present. For starters, just as the modern team is built on outsiders, born far from the confines of N5, so too was the original side of 1886, created by economic migrants from the Midlands, the North of England and Scotland, looking to prosper in London.

Of course, the history of Arsenal has been told myriad times. But the beauty of this book, and its use of *Daily Mirror* photographic and written archives, is that it allows us to dip into the past in a unique way.

In a sense it is a social history of Arsenal, providing a perspective of events in the context of the time they occurred, through

the newspaper cuttings that have been reproduced and the evocative, atmospheric photos depicting bygone eras.

The result, I hope, is a nostalgia-packed journey, taking you through the club's evolution from its beginnings as a south London munitions factory team, through the nurturing of some of the game's fabled characters – from notorious chairman Henry Norris to the great innovator Herbert Chapman, and the players from Brylcreem Boy Denis Compton, wee Alex James, Charlie George and Frank McLintock, up to the fresh-in-the-memory figures of Tony Adams and Ian Wright (perhaps the last bastion of a pre-modern Arsenal).

A line in the sand is drawn at the advent of the Premier League, when Arsenal, and football, were carried along on a wave of ruthless commercialism. The result is a book that is, above all, about a time when football was football – and it leaves you to decide which you prefer.

By Paul Joseph, author of When Football Was Football – Arsenal

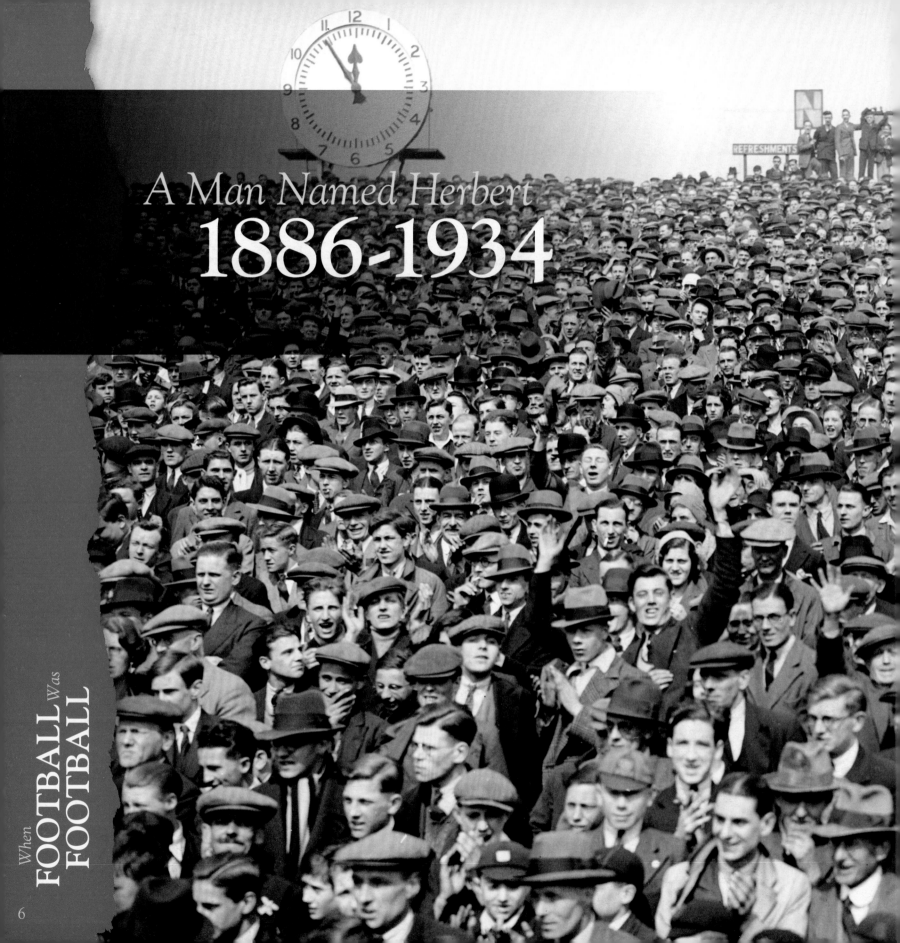

A Man Named Herbert
1886-1934

WAY HOME IS BY METRO FROM DRAYTON PK STN

The Clock End crowd watch Arsenal play Sheffield Wednesday
at Highbury, April 1933.

1886 Arsenal are founded as Dial Square by workers at the Royal Arsenal munitions factory in Woolwich, south London, and are renamed Royal Arsenal shortly after. 1886 Founding member David Danskin captains the team in their first match against Eastern Wanderers at Plumstead Common, which they win 6-0. 1888 The club begins playing matches at Manor Field in Plumstead, later renamed the Manor Ground. 1890 The club moves to the Invicta Ground in Plumstead. 1891 The club turns professional and renames itself Woolwich Arsenal. 1893 The club joins the Football League, starting out in the Second Division. 1897 Thomas Mitchell is appointed as the club's first professional manager. 1901 Harry Bradshaw is appointed manager. 1904 The club wins promotion to the First Division. 1910 Sir Henry Norris joins the club as majority shareholder. 1913 Soon after relegation back to the Second Division, the club moves to the new Arsenal Stadium in Highbury, north London. 1913 The club's first match at Highbury is a 2-1 victory against Leicester Fosse. 1914 The club drops the word "Woolwich" from its name to become "Arsenal". 1915 Football is suspended after the outbreak of the First World War. During the war, clubs in London combine with some Southern League teams to form a London Combination, in which Arsenal compete for the next four years. 1919 With the return of league football, Arsenal are elected to rejoin the First Division at the expense of north London neighbours Tottenham Hotspur. 1925 Arsenal appoint Herbert Chapman as manager. 1927 Arsenal lose the FA Cup final to Cardiff. 1929 Henry Norris is banned from football for life due to financial irregularities. 1930 Arsenal win their first major trophy – the FA Cup against Huddersfield Town. 1931 Arsenal win the league title for the first time. 1933 Arsenal win the league title. 1934 Chapman dies of pneumonia, but Arsenal go on to win a second consecutive league title under caretaker manager Joe Shaw. George Allison takes over permanently in the close season.

Left to right: Eddie Hapgood, Frank Moss, Alex James and Hapgood's son on the Highbury pitch, August 1934.

Royal Beginnings

Before Wenger's Arsenal, Graham's Arsenal, or even Chapman's Arsenal there was Royal Arsenal. Formed in 1886 – initially as Dial Square – by a group of workers at the Woolwich armaments factory in south London, Royal Arsenal remained the club's name until it turned professional in 1891 and swapped "Royal" for "Woolwich".

Since its inception the club had played matches at various sites in Plumstead, south London, before settling at the Manor Ground in 1893, made distinctive by a large open sewer down one side and a notoriously muddy pitch. There were no stands worthy of the description and the club used wagons borrowed from nearby army bases to house spectators. On such shoddy foundations it is little surprise the club struggled during its early years, flirting with relegation in 1910 and falling into financial trouble before eventually succumbing to the drop in 1913.

WOOLWICH TAKE THE FIELD.

In the first round of the English Cup Woolwich Arsenal met Fulham on Saturday on a wet and heavy ground. The Arsenal took the field a very fit team and well able, as the result proved, to realise the enthusiastic reception their supporters gave them.

20,000 CROWD WATCHING A LONDON FOOTBALL MATCH.

ABOVE One of the first football photographs to appear in the *Daily Mirror*, showing Woolwich Arsenal players entering the field at the Manor Ground before a match against Fulham in the Association Cup (now the FA Cup), February 1904.

LEFT A 20,000-strong crowd at the Manor Ground watching Woolwich Arsenal beat Derby County, also in the Association Cup, March 1906.

OPPOSITE Action from a match between Woolwich Arsenal and Tottenham Hotspur at White Hart Lane. The clubs were not yet neighbourhood rivals but found themselves in a battle against relegation during the 2009/10 season. Both survived to fight another day.

London Football Clubs' Struggle to Avoid Relegation.

Tottenham Hotspur and Woolwich Arsenal drew 1—1 at White Hart-lane on Saturday, and both teams are for the moment clear of the last two places in the League table, although Tottenham are not yet safe from the danger of relegation. (1) Joyce (Tottenham) saving. Note the spectators on the roof of the stand. (2) The Arsenal open the scoring. (3) Tottenham equalise.

Norris the Notorious

In 1913, with the club in serious financial trouble, chairman Sir Henry Norris hit on an idea to revive its fortunes: moving to a new stadium in a larger catchment area. The Arsenal Stadium in Highbury, north London, opened in 1913. But before Norris's masterplan had a chance to prosper, the First World War broke out. Arsenal played their last pre-war game on 24 April 1915, a 7-0 victory over Nottingham Forest. It would also be – at time of writing! – the club's last match outside the top flight of English football. During the war, Arsenal competed in a makeshift London Combination League, but with virtually every staff member contributing to the war effort, the club drafted in "guest" players to honour its fixtures.

Football's return to a conventional league format in

TO-DAY'S OPENING OF THE FOOTBALL SEASON.

Full Programme of Important Matches in Town and Country.

THE GAME'S BRIGHT PROSPECTS

To-day will see the opening of the first football season since the war, and, given anything like fine weather, huge crowds will assemble at all the big grounds. From all accounts greater interest than ever is to be taken in the winter game this season, and club managers are looking forward to the most successful season, in a financial sense, they have ever experienced.

Naturally it is difficult to estimate the prospects of the various clubs on this first Saturday of such a season. During the war years players have played for whichever club was nearest to their work or regimental station; now they automatically return to their own clubs, and in a great measure all teams are experimental.

Of course, the big clubs will have strong sides. Astute managers have been busy team building ever since the armistice, and such sides as Everton, Liverpool, Newcastle United, the Villa, Sunderland, the Sheffield, Manchester and Nottingham clubs, Chelsea, the Arsenal, the 'Spurs, West Ham, Fulham, to mention only a few, will certainly be as strong as they were before the war.

To attempt to forecast the probable results of to-day's games, however, is like taking a jump in the dark. The full list of important matches for to-day is as follows:—

1919 saw a surge of interest in the game. To reflect this renewed enthusiasm, expansion of the First and Second Divisions from 20 to 22 clubs was agreed by all parties. The problem was deciding how to gain the requisite number of clubs in each division in a fair manner. What followed has gone down in football folklore. Despite only finishing fifth in the Second Division the season before the war, Arsenal were elected to the top flight at the expense of Tottenham Hotspur, who were relegated having finished 20th in the First Division. The official line was that Arsenal had been rewarded for their "service and loyalty" to the league, but allegations of skullduggery have persisted. It is claimed that Norris bribed the voting members of the Football League, and although no firm proof has ever been offered, the tale marks the genesis of the enduring enmity between Arsenal and Tottenham.

Football for Wounded.—At the Arsenal v. Newcastle United match to-morrow at Highbury a limited number of the best seats in the grand stand will be reserved free for wounded soldiers who apply before 2.45 p.m.

Leslie Knighton's reign as Arsenal manager was unremarkable on the pitch and tumultuous off it. During his six-year tenure between 1919 and 1925, the club finished no higher than mid-table. He also had numerous fallings-out with chairman Norris, who put a strict cap of £1,000 on transfer fees and refused to sign any player under 5ft 8in tall or 11 stone in weight. Despite the chairman's meddling, Knighton signed several gifted players including Bob John, Jimmy Brain and Alf Baker, all of whom would play vital roles in Arsenal's early success in the 1930s.

During his final season at Arsenal, Knighton was involved in one of the first recorded cases of doping. Before a game against West Ham, he told his players to swallow pills given to him by a Harley Street doctor. Although the pills increased energy levels, the side-effects – including raging thirst – were less desirable.

Knighton's activities, entirely legal under the rules at the time, were revealed only later in his memoirs. Norris dismissed Knighton in the summer of 1925 after a poor season which saw Arsenal narrowly avoid relegation. The hunt was on for his successor – but not just any successor.

ARSENAL AND THEIR MANAGER

Mr. Leslie Knighton to Leave the Highbury Club

Mr. Leslie Knighton, manager of the Arsenal Football Club, and his directors have not seen eye to eye in the conduct of the club's affairs, and have decided to part company on terms of mutual respect.

Mr. Knighton left Manchester City for Highbury six years ago, and during his term of office the club has held its position in the First Division of the League, in spite of much misfortune in the matter of accidents to players.

During the past season Robson was ill with diphtheria, and Milne, Donald Cock and Kennedy all had broken limbs, and yet the club, if failing to maintain its early promise, managed to make itself secure.

> *Arsenal Football Club is open to receive applications for the position of TEAM MANAGER. He must be experienced and possess the highest qualifications for the post, both as to ability and personal character. Gentlemen whose sole ability to build up a good side depends on the payment of heavy and exhorbitant [sic] transfer fees need not apply.*

A newspaper advert placed by Henry Norris after the sacking of Leslie Knighton. With the club strapped for cash, the chairman emphasized the need for a coach who could operate without big-money signings.

Coaxing Yorkshire-born Herbert Chapman down south to manage Arsenal was a major coup for Norris and an epochal moment in the club's history. Chapman had just won the league title for a second season running with Huddersfield Town, and in the summer of 1925 was bolstering his squad in preparation for a shot at three in a row (which had never been achieved before). But the challenge of reviving an underachieving Arsenal – plus a significant salary increase – was enough to lure Chapman away.

One of his first moves was to sign the 34-year-old England international Charlie Buchan, whom he made Arsenal captain. Chapman and Buchan's arrivals coincided with a change in the offside law that reduced the number of opposition players that an attacker needed between himself and the goal-line from three to two (including the goalkeeper).

Buchan's idea, implemented by Chapman, was to move the roaming centre-half Jack Butler back from midfield to a "stopper" position in defence. The inside forwards would also be given more defensive duties, effectively creating a 3–4–3, or a "WM" formation, named as such because of the similarities with the shape formed by the letters. Many condemned it as a negative strategy – but few could argue with the results it yielded.

> "At Arsenal Stadium we don't sign players for special positions – we sign footballers who can do their job anywhere."
> Herbert Chapman

Mr. H Ch[...]

C. Buchan.

BUCHAN FOR THE ARSENAL

Sunderland Wizard To Be Seen with the Gunners Next Season

A big sensation was created yesterday when it was announced that Charles Buchan, the Sunderland wizard, had signed for the Arsenal.

Buchan is of London birth, so that really he is but coming home. Graduating with Leyton, he went to Sunderland fourteen years ago. He has been "capped" once against Scotland, twice against Wales and once against Ireland, in addition to which he has played against Belgium and France, and also took part in the Victory international against Wales.

Herbie Roberts (right) helps to greet new signing George Drury at Highbury, March 1938. Roberts replaced Jack Butler as the "stopper" in Chapman's WM formation. His reputation for nullifying the opposition's centre-forward made him one of the most unpopular players in the country and he was regularly barracked at away games. He played 335 games for Arsenal.

The 1927 FA Cup Final

One of Chapman's opening pledges was to have Arsenal challenging for trophies within five years. In his first season they finished second, five points behind his old side Huddersfield Town – who won their third title in a row – and the five-year project looked to be ahead of schedule. But this proved to be a false dawn and Arsenal spent most of the remaining decade in mid-table.

Despite the chairman's appeal for a frugal manager, Chapman was not shy about dipping into the transfer market. In February 1926, he signed the winger Joe Hulme – said to be the fastest man in the game – followed that summer by forward Jack Lambert and full-back Tom Parker, who would later succeed Buchan as captain. Despite their patchy league form, in 1927 they reached the FA Cup final for the first time, but lost 1-0 to underdogs Cardiff City after an error by goalkeeper Dan Lewis. The lack of friction on his shiny new jersey was blamed for allowing the ball to slip through, and ever since that game Arsenal's goalkeepers' tops have always been washed before use.

C. Buchan, captain of Arsenal.

F. Keenor, Cardiff City's captain.

All is ready for the great F.A. Cup Final between Arsenal and Cardiff City, which the King is to attend at Wembley to-day. Weather prospects are hopeful. Would-be spectators are warned that it is useless for anyone not in possession of a ticket to seek admission to the Stadium, as all accommodation has been allotted. A running commentary of the game will be broadcast. See also pages 10 and 11.

The Arsenal squad of 1927.

Captain Charles Buchan shakes hands with his Cardiff counterpart Fred Keenor before the game at Wembley Stadium, April 1927.

Dan Lewis fumbles a shot from Cardiff's Hughie Ferguson and the ball trickles over the line for Cardiff's winner.

Norris Resigns

The summer following defeat to Cardiff, Arsenal became embroiled in a scandal. Footballers' pay at the time was limited by a maximum wage, but an FA enquiry found that Charlie Buchan had secretly received illegal payments from Arsenal as an incentive to sign for the club. Perhaps pre-empting the verdict, Henry Norris resigned as chairman and was replaced by Samuel Hill-Wood, a former cricketer and Conservative politician. For Norris, it was the end of his involvement in football as the FA banned him from the game for life. But for Chapman, the departure of the autocratic Norris meant the reins were off and he was now free to explore his unique vision for the club.

The match programme for the Cup final.

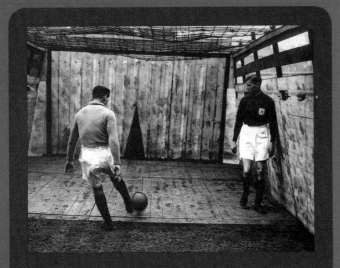

Charles Buchan and goalkeeper Dan Lewis preparing for the FA Cup final in what appears to be a rickety garden shed, April 1927.

Welsh defender Bob John, who consoled his tear-stricken compatriot Dan Lewis after the game, promising him he would get another chance to win a medal (a promise that would remain unfulfilled). Renowned for his distribution and ball-winning abilities, John played 470 games for Arsenal.

> " If this match had to be replayed tomorrow, Lewis would still be my first choice for goal. "
> Herbert Chapman

1930 Arsenal's First Trophy

20,000 NEW SEATS FOR CUP FINAL SPECTATORS

Fixing some of the 20,000 new seats at Wembley Stadium in preparation for the Cup Final between Arsenal and Huddersfield Town, to be played to-morrow.

BELOW Alex James scores against Huddersfield Town in the FA Cup final at Wembley, April 1930. Right on cue, five years after Chapman's arrival, Arsenal had landed their first ever trophy.

OPPOSITE An enduring memory from the 1930 final is the sinister image of the *Graf Zeppelin* looming over the stadium during the first half. The presence of the German airship was jeered by fans of both teams, who thought it might distract the players.

1931
Arsenal's First League Title

A year after victory in the FA Cup, Arsenal secured their first league title, and they did it in style, setting a new points total which would not be bettered for 30 years. A formidable front line of Jack Lambert, David Jack and Cliff Bastin was too much for opposition defences who were unable to cope with their combined talents.

ARSENAL DO IT

Lambert (dark shirt), who scored Arsenal's third goal, tries to break through.

Members of the Arsenal first and second teams with trophies they have won, including the Sheriff of London's Shield, the League Cup, the Northampton Hospital Shield, the London Combination Cup and the F.A. Charity Shield.

TOP RIGHT A *Daily Mirror* cutting showing action from the match that secured Arsenal their first league title, a 3-1 victory over Liverpool at Highbury, April 1931.

LEFT Jack Lambert, top scorer during Arsenal's 1931 title-winning campaign.

ABOVE Arsenal players and officials board an Imperial Airways flight at Croydon in October 1932, en route to Paris to play the Paris Racing Club in a charity game to raise money for war invalids.

1932
The Over-the-Line Final

The 1932 FA Cup final between Arsenal and Newcastle is memorable for the goal that wasn't a goal, and the player who didn't play. Arsenal had led 1-0 through a Bob John goal, when Newcastle equalized after a long ball had appeared to go out for a goal kick. Winger Jimmy Richardson crossed the ball back into play and Jack Allen levelled things up. Allen scored again in the second half to win the match 2-1. The incident sparked discussion over the need for line judges to avoid such controversies – a precursor to the modern day debate over video technology. But equally significant was the absence of Alex James from the Arsenal line-up at Wembley that day – the midfield magician had injured himself in a pre-match press photocall. Without him Arsenal just weren't the same side.

FILM PROVES THE BALL WAS OUT OF PLAY
NEWCASTLE'S LUCKY EQUALISER IN CUP FINAL

TOP A still from the British Movietone film of the Cup final, purporting to show that the ball had gone out of play in the build-up to Newcastle's equalizer. The dotted lines indicate the angles of vision of referee and linesmen, suggesting they were poorly placed to make the call.

ABOVE Newcastle on the attack at Wembley.

–LEGENDS–

David Jack

Concerns over extravagant transfer fees are not entirely new. When Arsenal signed Bolton's David Jack for £10,890 in 1928 it was the first time a footballer had ever been transferred for more than £10,000. Sir Charles Clegg, President of the Football Association, claimed that no player in the world was worth that amount of money, whilst others simply considered the 29-year-old past his best.

Over the next six years the Lancashire-born forward proved himself value for money, and then some. He recorded a personal best of 34 goals in Arsenal's championship-winning season of 1930/31, and won two more league titles in 1932/33 and 1933/34. He also boasts the accolade of being the first ever Arsenal player to captain England. Cocking a snoop at those who doubted his worth, Chapman later said that buying Jack was "one of the best bargains I ever made".

FOOTBALL –STATS–

David Jack

Name: David Bone Nightingale Jack

Born: 1899

Died: 1958

Playing Career: 1919-1934

Clubs: Plymouth Argyle, Bolton Wanderers, Arsenal

Arsenal Appearances: 208

Goals: 124

England Appearances: 9

Goals: 3

Managerial Career: Southend United, Middlesbrough, Shelbourne

Lucky Arsenal?

During Arsenal's gilded age of the 1930s, their ability to grab goals on the counter-attack, by soaking up pressure and then breaking quickly, led some observers to dub them "lucky".

The tag irritated many at the club who were proud of their tactical approach and the rewards it reaped. Cliff Bastin even used his *Daily Mirror* column, opposite, to debunk the myth that Arsenal were in cahoots with the gods of football. "Hasn't it ever occurred to our critics that we intend to win that way?" he wrote. Nevertheless, the mud stuck and the phrase "lucky Arsenal" became part of the football lexicon.

LUCKY ARSENAL WIN

LUCKY ARSENAL STILL IN THE HUNT

LUCKY ARSENAL!

'LUCKY' ARSENAL LOSE AGAIN

THE LUCK OF OLD ARSENAL

" *At Highbury we went for results. Results meant getting goals so we cut the movements down from four passes to two. Our great ball was the long one and that opened the game up.* "

Ted Drake

Ted Drake, scorer of 124 "lucky" Arsenal goals.

Schemes, Not Tricks, Needed to Make Football's Super-Teams

OUR FAMOUS "POW-WOW"

Duel of Tactics Likely in Clash with Spurs—Be Prepared for Changes!

By CLIFFORD BASTIN (Arsenal and England)

"ARSENAL were lucky to win. The other side were attacking three parts of the time." Whenever I read or hear that, and it happens pretty often, I become mildly annoyed. It's unfair to us.

As often as not, I admit, the other team has more of the midfield play, or at any rate appears to do so. As often as not our goals are scored from a few breakaways.

That's how a big proportion of our matches are won. But hasn't it ever occurred to our critics that we mean to win that way?

A lot has been said and written about our success being due, in great part, to our rule of meeting the day before a match for a general pow-wow. How many people, I wonder, appreciate that what they see next day on the field of play is just what we have schemed for?

We run over the personnel of the team we are to meet. What's-his-name, one of their inside forwards, is known to be dangerous if he has half a yard to move in, so one of our wing halves is told off to see that he never gets that half-yard.

That nips 50 per cent. of their best movements in the bud before the game has started. So-and-so is a through-pass expert. We are constantly on the watch to intercept those passes.

Simple, but Effective

As for our own attack, many of you will have noticed that our opponents may be attacking strongly when suddenly the ball comes out to Alex James. He puts it hard across to Joe Hulme, who uses his exceptional speed to get it to the other end of the field in the shortest possible time. It comes across to me, maybe, and I, knowing beforehand what to expect, am ready for it. Simple, but effective, as we have found in match after match.

After this "lucky" goal, our opponents attack for another long period, what time we forwards do little work. Consequently, we are seldom run to a standstill, and especially towards the end of a game we are likely to be fresher than the other fellows. Our brains and, I might add, Mr. Chapman's, have saved our legs.

Very likely as individuals the other side are as good as ourselves. Some people might say their football is more attractive to watch. But remember that a football team goes on to the field to score more goals than its opponents and is justified in using any tactics, as long as they are clean. We can claim, at any rate, that our methods bring results.

Here is one outstanding example. In our Cup Semi-Final with Manchester City two years ago, Manchester seemed to be attacking all the time.

A few minutes from the end a long kick up the field reached Lambert, who chased the ball hard.

Possibly the full back should have cleared, but Lambert got to it and put it across to me without pausing to look. He knew that I was in the centre waiting for it. Result—a "lucky" scoring shot.

gerous. The Wolves won that day by a goal to nothing.

In the match at Tottenham a fortnight or so ago, Nelson, the Wolves' centre-half, played an attacking game throughout, which left Hunt with plenty of room. The Spurs' forwards tumbled to this in the second half, and Hunt seized the opportunity to score twice.

In the return match the centre half was on top of Hunt all the time, and the spear-head of the Spurs' attack was blunted and all but useless. Which only goes to prove that it pays to think about your opponents before you meet them on the field.

So with many other teams. I don't often get the chance to watch other people's matches, but when I read about these "fluke" wins I often suspect that the winners have merely used their brains a bit and been content to let the losers do the flashy things in midfield.

A New Angle

One thing is certain. No teams get to the top and stay there without playing according to a well-rehearsed plan. The clever tricks come as second nature to a man who has played first-class football for a long time. More than that is needed to make a super-team.

For that reason our game next Saturday with the Spurs should be more than an ordinary local Derby. They are at the top of the First Division, and by all accounts got there by good football.

They won't forget to try to evolve some plan to stop our own schemes from bearing fruit. We, on the other hand, shall have made just as careful a study of their methods. So the man who goes to Tottenham with an eye wide open for tactics may find that the game has an altogether new interest for him.

He may even notice that after half-time we, or they, or both of us, will have changed our plans. It's quite a useful angle from which to watch a game and a new one for most people, I fancy.

Our Scottish "Holiday"

I am looking forward to our match next Wednesday with Glasgow Rangers. Those who can be there will see a marked contrast in style—the Scots, with their intricate close-passing game, which they play to perfection, and which is fascinating to watch; and our English style, which, so some think, looks crude by comparison.

Our opponents, however, will find that it is built up on more than sheer speed. If we win we shall feel that we have vindicated English methods in the stronghold of Scottish Soccer.

It ought to be a pleasant holiday for us, for we leave for Scotland on Sunday, play the Rangers at golf on Monday, and meet them at football at the Ibrox ground two days later, returning that night and arriving in London on Thursday morning.

A professional footballer's life has its compensations, you see!

LEGENDS

Alex James

If someone were to draw a prototype of a football genius, it's unlikely that Alex James would be used as a template. Short, stocky and a wearer of trademark baggy shorts (to hide the long johns that protected against his rheumatism), the Scot signed for Arsenal from Preston in 1927 and became a pivotal figure in the club's domination of the 1930s. Playing as a deep-lying midfielder he scored relatively few goals, but created many. His creativity and intelligence made him the perfect foil for the likes of Cliff Bastin, Ted Drake and David Jack, whose goalscoring feats owed a great debt to wee Alex.

Surprisingly, he won just eight caps for Scotland, partly because of Preston's reluctance to release him for internationals. However, he did appear for the legendary "Wembley Wizards" team that demolished England 5-1 at Wembley in 1928, with James scoring twice. During the Second World War he served in the Royal Artillery, and after the war became a journalist. In 1949 he returned to Arsenal to coach the club's youth sides, before his sudden death from cancer four years later, aged 51.

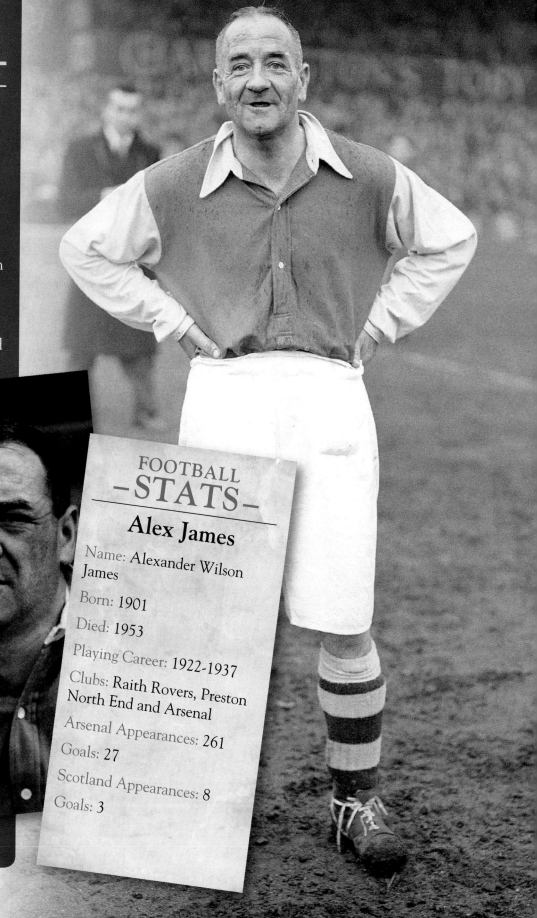

FOOTBALL STATS

Alex James

Name: Alexander Wilson James

Born: 1901

Died: 1953

Playing Career: 1922-1937

Clubs: Raith Rovers, Preston North End and Arsenal

Arsenal Appearances: 261

Goals: 27

Scotland Appearances: 8

Goals: 3

1933-1934 The Reds Go Marching On

Undeterred by Arsenal's 1932 Cup final defeat, Chapman kept faith with his side and set about challenging for the league title the following season. A humiliating FA Cup exit at the hands of Walsall of the Third Division was a temporary glitch, mitigated by the absence of five first team players through injury or flu. Ultimately Arsenal would show their class, ending the campaign as champions, scoring an impressive 118 league goals along the way.

Wary of his ageing team and the club's inadequate reserves (as proven by the Walsall match), Chapman was keen to bring in fresh blood. For the 1933/34 season he signed Ray Bowden, Pat Beasley and Jimmy Dunne, and converted the young George Male from left-half to right-back. Yet he would not live to see the end of the season, let alone complete the task of rebuilding his side. A goalless draw with Birmingham City on 30 December 1933 proved to be Chapman's last match in charge.

HIGHEST-EVER SEAT BOOKINGS

8 Matches in a Month for Champions

THAT "DOUBLE"

ARSENAL'S RECORD START TO SEASON

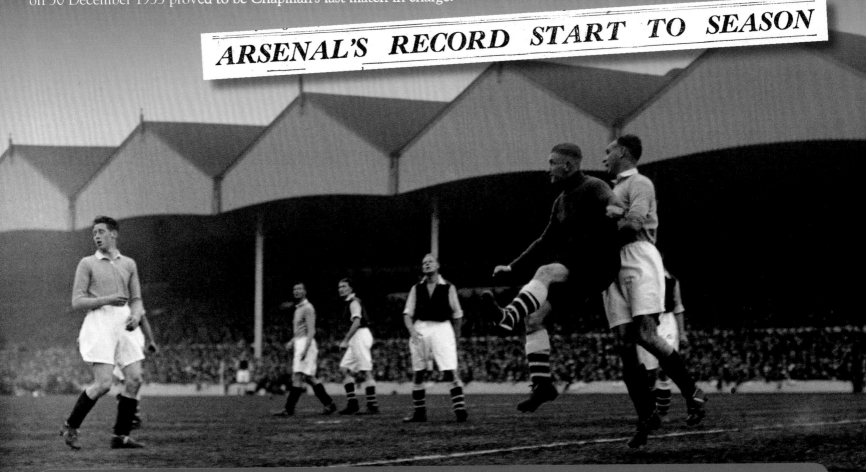

Arsenal goalkeeper Frank Moss clears the ball during a match against Glasgow Rangers at Highbury, September 1934. Between 1933 and 1967 Arsenal and Rangers played each other regularly, and the match became known as the Battle of Britain. The bond between the clubs was born of the close friendship between Herbert Chapman and his Rangers counterpart Bill Struth.

The Great Man Passes

RIGHT A crowd including players and fans lined the streets outside the church. Chapman died of pneumonia just days after travelling up north on a scouting trip.

Arsenal players forming a guard of honour.

The Empty Seat.—A dramatic picture showing the seat occupied by Mr. Herbert Chapman for many years, and from which he directed the Arsenal's matches. It was taken while the crowd was observing silence during the Last Post in his memory at Highbury on Saturday.

(A to B) : James, Hapgood, Hulme and Jack, who were among players to come up from training at Brighton.

–LEGENDS–

Herbert Chapman

Like so many other coaching greats, Chapman's playing career was unexceptional, with less than 40 league appearances to his name. But in management he found his true calling. After gaining success with Northampton Town, Leeds City and most notably Huddersfield Town, he found the challenge of rejuvenating a postwar Arsenal too attractive to turn down. He transformed the club, making them the dominant team of the 1930s, and left an indelible mark not only on Arsenal, but on football.

Chapman was one of the game's first modernizers, introducing pioneering tactics, but also a fresh vision for how a football club should be run from top to bottom. He was responsible for a number of groundbreaking innovations that today we take for granted. Floodlights, numbered shirts, and the renaming of Gillespie Road tube station to "Arsenal" are just some of the legacies he left. He also understood the importance of PR, and initiated the tradition of Arsenal players clapping all four corners of the ground on entering the pitch before games.

> " *He should have been prime minister.* "
> Cliff Bastin

FOOTBALL –STATS–

Herbert Chapman

Name: Herbert Chapman
Born: 1874
Died: 1934
Playing Career: 1895-1909
Clubs: Ashton North End, Stalybridge Rovers, Rochdale, Grimsby Town, Swindon Town, Sheppey United, Worksop Town, Northampton Town (twice), Sheffield United, Notts County, Tottenham Hotspur
Club Appearances: 100+
Goals: 40+
Managerial Career: Northampton Town, Leeds City, Huddersfield Town, Arsenal

CHAPMAN: Legend

ABOVE The bronze bust of Chapman, sculpted by Jacob Epstein, that resided inside the marble halls of Highbury.

Glory Interrupted
1935-1945

When
FOOTBALL Was
FOOTBALL

A game against Dynamo Moscow, played in thick fog at Tottenham Hotspurs' White Hart Lane Stadium as part of a goodwill visit to the United Kingdom, November 1945. During the Great War, Tottenham had used Highbury for some of their "home" games and the favour was returned in the Second World War as Arsenal converted its stadium

1935 Highbury's largest ever crowd of 73,295 witnesses a 0-0 draw against Sunderland. **1935** Arsenal win a third consecutive league title **1936** Arsenal win the FA Cup against Sheffield United. **1936** Highbury's art deco East Stand is opened. **1938** Arsenal win the league title. **1938** England play Italy in a violent "friendly" in what becomes known as the Battle of Highbury. **1939** Competitive professional football is suspended following the outbreak of the Second World War. Arsenal closes its stadium to football and converts it into an ARP centre. **1940** A bomb falls near Highbury Stadium, killing two RAF men sitting in a hut. **1940** Arsenal win the League South 'A' title. **1941** Highbury is bombed once more, with the stadium taking a direct hit. The North Bank is wrecked after a fire breaks out and the roof collapses. **1941** Arsenal and Preston draw the Football League War Cup 1-1 at Wembley Stadium. Arsenal lose the replay 2-1. **1942** Arsenal win the breakaway London League. **1943** Arsenal mark their return to the Football League South by winning the championship and the League South Cup.

Bryn Jones, following his transfer from Wolverhampton Wanderers to Arsenal for a world record fee of £14,000, August 1938. With the effects of the Great Depression still being felt in Britain and beyond, the transfer led to questions being asked in the House of Commons about its appropriateness.

Life After Chapman

Following Chapman's sudden death, caretaker manager Joe Shaw seamlessly continued his work by leading Arsenal to their second title in a row in 1934. A season later, under newly appointed full-time successor George Allison, they made it an historic hat-trick. In contrast to his predecessor, Allison took a hands-off approach to management and was rarely seen on the training pitch.

On paper his trophy haul remains impressive – he won the FA Cup in the 1935/36 season and the league again in 1937/38 – but arguably his limitations were exposed when the time came to rebuild the side created by Chapman. Allison was unable to adequately replace many of the stars from the first half of the decade. He was also robbed of the time to do so by the outbreak of the Second World War.

LEFT George Allison in his Highbury office. Allison, an experienced journalist and the first to obtain an interview with British Field Marshall Lord Kitchener, began his association with Arsenal as editor of the club's match day programme.

BELOW LEFT Arsenal goalkeeper Moss comes out to save from Sunderland's Gurney in a match watched by 73,295, Highbury's largest ever attendance, March 1935.

DRAKE SETTLES IT FOR GUNNERS

Goal in Sixth Minute Brings Win and Championship

BY A SPECIAL CORRESPONDENT

Edward Drake, the season's leading goalscorer, gave Arsenal victory and the League championship at Middlesbrough yesterday, where Arsenal won 1—0.

Arsenal in 1904 —And Now!

FAMOUS CLUB'S AMAZING GROWTH

In 1904, Arsenal Football Club, then playing at Plumstead, reported a "record" amount in gate receipts of £8,461.

Last night shareholders at the annual general meeting in London, passed the statement of accounts showing that £68,827 was taken in gate receipts during 1933-34.

The 1904 balance-sheet, in possession of one of the oldest shareholders of the club, pointed out that £540 was paid for transfer of players, "it having become necessary to secure some new players of the very best class."

Sir Samuel Hill-Wood, chairman of the meeting, mentioned that £17,313 more had been spent on new players last season than the previous one

Unconsciously reiterating the declared policy contained in the 1904 report, Sir Samuel said: "We have been going through a very difficult time with players growing old. We all realise the only policy of Arsenal is to be on top, and therefore we have to replace players, always remembering our motto that 'only the best is good enough.'"

TRIBUTE TO PLAYERS

The chairman, who revealed that £16,147 was paid in entertainment tax during the 1933-34 season, paid a tribute to the staff and players for pulling themselves together after the great loss sustained by the death of Mr. Herbert Chapman, the late manager, and for going on to win the championship.

After £11,000 transferred to reserve for income tax payments, £10,000 written off for ground expenditure, and a certain sum for transfer fees which may become payable, the club showed a balance on last season's working of £774.

The meeting paid a tribute to the memories of Mr. Herbert Chapman, Mr. Langham Reed, a former director, and Sir Henry Norris, who died yesterday. Sir Henry was at one time a chairman of the club.

Colonel Sir Mathew Wilson, Bart., and Major-General McLachlan were re-elected directors.

Chapman's Legacy

This cutting illustrates the changing fortunes of the club since the start of the decade. Thanks to the late Chapman, Arsenal were now the best known and richest club in the country, and the balance sheets reflected their lofty status.

TRUE, BY JAMES!

True tale from Wardour-street yesterday:

The Jubilee film, "Drake of England," is being cold-shouldered by some cinema exhibitors in the north because they consider the title suggests more Arsenal publicity.

ABOVE Evidence that football fan paranoia has been around for decades.

BELOW Even in 1935 Tottenham were the butt of jokes.

35

–LEGENDS–

Cliff Bastin

Boy Bastin, known as such because of his precocious talent as a youngster, started his career at Exeter City aged just 16. He was soon spotted by Herbert Chapman, and although he had played a mere 17 times for the Devon club, Chapman was so impressed he signed him at the end of the 1928/29 season.

Despite his age, Bastin showed a remarkable coolness and deadly precision in front of goal. He was Arsenal's all-time top goalscorer from 1939 until 1997 – all the more impressive since he played, notionally at least, on the left wing rather than as centre-forward. In reality he was as much a striker as a winger, with Arsenal's tactics requiring their wide-men to cut into the penalty box at regular intervals. Injuries sidelined Bastin towards the end of the 1930s before the outbreak of the Second World War truncated his career.

Bastin was excused military service after failing the army hearing test (he was in fact rapidly going deaf), and instead served as an ARP Officer, stationed on top of Highbury Stadium. In 1941, a propaganda broadcast in Fascist Italy spuriously claimed that Bastin had been captured in the Battle of Crete, despite being ensconced at Highbury. After retirement, Bastin returned to his native Exeter and ran a pub. He died in 1991.

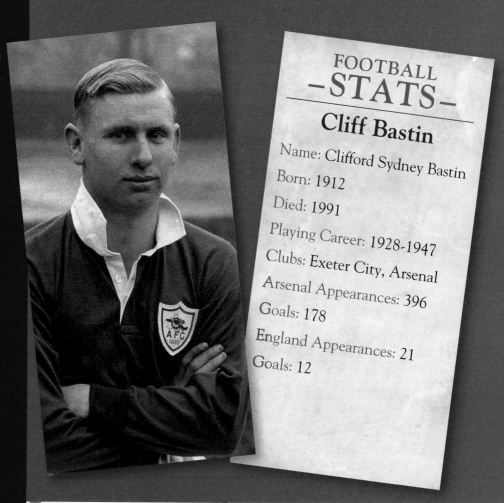

FOOTBALL –STATS–

Cliff Bastin

Name: Clifford Sydney Bastin

Born: 1912

Died: 1991

Playing Career: 1928-1947

Clubs: Exeter City, Arsenal

Arsenal Appearances: 396

Goals: 178

England Appearances: 21

Goals: 12

Clockwise from left, England footballers Cliff Bastin, Ted Drake, Alf Young, Tom Whittaker, Ken Willingham and Eddie Hapgood on board a ship sailing for an England game abroad, 1938.

ABOVE Alex James parades the pitch holding the FA Cup after victory over Sheffield United in the 1936 final, while team-mate Joe Hulme attempts to untangle himself from a police officer. Arsenal won by a single goal, scored by Ted Drake. A dispute over filming rights meant that newsreels for the game were banned; consequently only aerial shots exist.

OPPOSITE Arsenal captain Alex James holds the cup aloft.

LEFT Bremner, Arsenal's inside-right, evades the challenge of a Bolton player during a 5-0 victory that secured Arsenal the 1937/38 league title – their fifth in seven years. However, the near-invincible team which had dominated the decade was generally considered to be in decline.

ABOVE Bryan Jones prepares to cross during a match at Highbury, August 1938.

OPPOSITE Eddie Hapgood with his son at Highbury, August 1934.

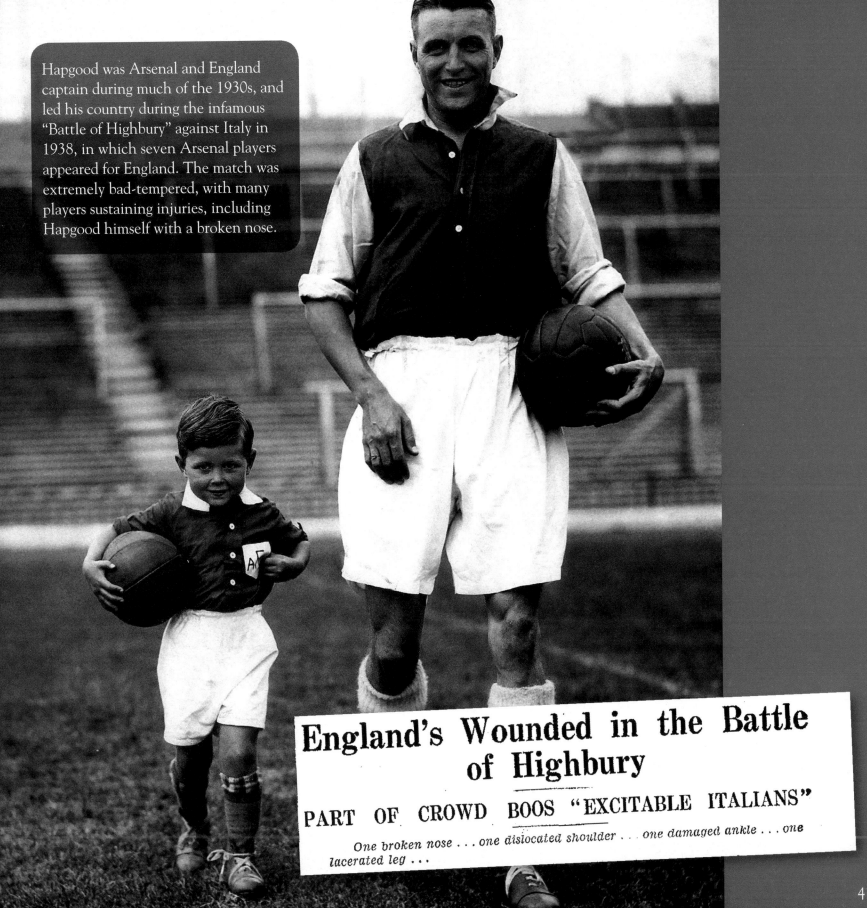

Hapgood was Arsenal and England captain during much of the 1930s, and led his country during the infamous "Battle of Highbury" against Italy in 1938, in which seven Arsenal players appeared for England. The match was extremely bad-tempered, with many players sustaining injuries, including Hapgood himself with a broken nose.

England's Wounded in the Battle of Highbury

PART OF CROWD BOOS "EXCITABLE ITALIANS"

One broken nose . . . one dislocated shoulder . . . one damaged ankle . . . one lacerated leg . . .

–LEGENDS–

Ted Drake

Ted Drake's original vocation was that of a gas-meter reader, and he continued in this comparatively unglamorous line of work while playing youth football for Winchester City. His first professional club was Southampton, and after only one full season, in which he scored 20 goals, his power and goalscoring had attracted the attention of Herbert Chapman. Surprisingly, Drake rejected the chance of a move to Highbury and decided to remain on the south coast.

After Chapman's death, and with George Allison now in charge, Arsenal finally got their man in March 1934 for a fee of £6,500. Drake would go on to win two league titles and an FA Cup at Highbury – a personal highlight being a seven-goal performance against Aston Villa in 1935 – before the Second World War curtailed his career. He still managed to combine his duties in the Royal Air Force with turning out for Arsenal in wartime games, but by peacetime a spinal injury had forced him to retire from playing. He later became a manager, and while in charge of Chelsea he took the club to its only league title of the 20th century, becoming the first man to win the championship as a player and a manager.

> " Ted Drake was a big man with a big heart. The word profligacy didn't feature in his vocabulary. "
>
> Stanley Matthews

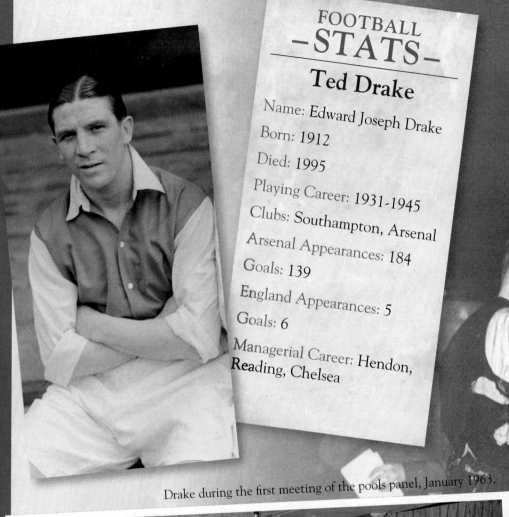

FOOTBALL
–STATS–
Ted Drake

Name: Edward Joseph Drake

Born: 1912

Died: 1995

Playing Career: 1931-1945

Clubs: Southampton, Arsenal

Arsenal Appearances: 184

Goals: 139

England Appearances: 5

Goals: 6

Managerial Career: Hendon, Reading, Chelsea

Drake during the first meeting of the pools panel, January 1963.

ED DRAKE   ARTHUR ELLIS   TOM FINNEY   TOMMY LAWTON   GEORGE YOUNG

As was the case during the Great War, guest players were required during the Second World War to help clubs whose staff were taking part in the war effort. Arsenal were represented by a number of high-profile names including Stanley Matthews, Stan Mortensen and Bill Shankly. Despite Highbury being used as an ARP centre, it was bombed in 1941. The North Bank was wrecked after a fire broke out and the roof collapsed, while the goalposts in front of the North Bank were also demolished. Much of the terracing on the South Stand was damaged too, and these had to be repaired before Arsenal could return home after the war.

When it was safe to play, Arsenal were one of the leading sides. They won the League South 'A' title in 1939/40 but lost the League War Cup final to Preston North End the following season. In 1941/42 a number of London clubs formed a breakaway London League and Arsenal romped to the title, scoring 108 goals in 30 matches. They returned to the Football League South a season later, winning the championship and the League South Cup.

ABOVE Dismantling of bunks in Finsbury Park tube station, a short walk from Highbury, at the end of the war, April 1945. During the hostilities, Islington residents took shelter here and in the Arsenal Underground station.

RIGHT Reg Lewis, who broke into the first team in the seasons proceeding the war and continued to be a regular during the conflict. His scoring tally including war games was a stunning 392 goals in 451 games, making him unofficially the most prolific goalscorer in the club's history.

New Foundations
1946-1967

A snowstorm interrupts a match at Highbury, circa 1967.

> "Football is no longer a game, no longer a sport. It is a business, ruthless business, where money dominates everything.
>
> Leo Horn – referee"

1946 Competitive professional football resumes following the end of the war. **1947** Arsenal are almost relegated from the top division before rallying to finish 13th. **1948** Following George Allison's retirement, Tom Whittaker is appointed secretary-manager and leads Arsenal to the league title. **1950** Arsenal win the FA Cup against Liverpool. **1952** Arsenal win the league title. **1953** Arsenal retain the league title, finishing level on points with Preston, but victorious on goal average by 0.999 of a goal. **1956** Jack Crayston is appointed manager following the sudden death of Tom Whittaker. **1958** Crayston resigns as manager and is replaced by George Swindin. **1962** Swindin resigns as manager and is replaced by Billy Wright. **1962** Denis Hill-Wood is appointed chairman. **1966** Bertie Mee is appointed manager following the sacking of Billy Wright.

Goalkeeper Ted Platt dives to make a save, November 1949.

Arsenal after the War

Whilst many of the club's personnel returned to action after the war, including manager George Allison, the four-year hiatus had taken its toll. With lynchpins Cliff Bastin and Ted Drake now retired, Arsenal finished the 1946/47 season in a lowly 13th place. It was enough to convince Allison to call it a day. In his place came Tom Whittaker, who had been associated with the club since 1919, first as a player, then physiotherapist, then assistant coach. If there were any doubts about his capacity to fill the hot seat, they were answered within a season as he led Arsenal to their first league title since before the war.

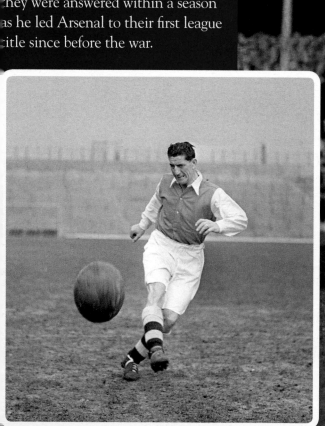

TOP RIGHT George Allison's replacement, Tom Whittaker.

LEFT Striker Ronnie Rooke, whose 33 goals propelled Arsenal to the 1947/48 league title.

ABOVE Goalkeeper George Swindin punches the ball clear during a match against Portsmouth at Highbury, October 1947. Like Ronnie Rooke, Swindin played in every game that season.

The Brylcreem Boy

Nowadays it's hard to imagine a player combining two sporting careers, but Denis Compton was an eminent Middlesex cricketer first and a footballer second. His spell at Arsenal – the only club he played for – was cut short by injury and he managed only 60 appearances. During the 1940s he also became a national icon as the public face of the Brylcreem range of men's haircare products.

–LEGENDS–

Jimmy Logie

Almost before he was able to kick a ball in anger Jimmy Logie's Arsenal career was interrupted by the Second World War. Logie served in the Royal Navy for the entire duration of the conflict. After being demobbed he rejoined Arsenal, playing several wartime matches before making his competitive debut in 1946. The gifted Scot was often compared to Alex James, and for the next eight seasons he was a regular in the Arsenal side, playing at inside-forward.

He took part in all the club's early postwar successes, including two league titles and the 1950 FA Cup – setting up both goals in a 2-0 win over Liverpool in the final. Despite his achievements at club level, Logie won only a single A cap for Scotland. After retirement he fell on hard times, got into gambling trouble, and worked in a newsagents in Piccadilly Circus before his death aged 64.

FOOTBALL –STATS–

Jimmy Logie

Name: James Tullis Logie

Born: 1919

Died: 1984

Playing Career: 1939-1960

Clubs: Arsenal, Gravesend & Northfleet

Arsenal Appearances: 296

Goals: 68

Scotland Appearances: 1

Managerial Career: Gravesend & Northfleet

The 1950 FA Cup Final

Arsenal achieved their third FA Cup success with a 2-0 victory over Liverpool. A brace by forward Reg Lewis won most of the plaudits, but it was captain Joe Mercer who put in perhaps his finest performance for the club. Mercer had enjoyed a fine season and his display at Wembley was its zenith. Bizarrely, during the build-up to the final, he had trained with opponents Liverpool as he still lived in the area following his move down south from neighbours Everton – though Liverpool were smart enough to ensure he sat out sessions directly relating to the big day.

ABOVE Arsenal players parade the Wembley pitch with the FA Cup after beating Liverpool.

LEFT Skipper Joe Mercer celebrates by drinking champagne from the trophy.

BACKGROUND Players in the victorious dressing room after the match.

–LEGENDS–

Joe Mercer

When Mercer arrived at Highbury from Everton in 1946, Arsenal were bottom of the First Division. Within a year the bow-legged left-half had helped galvanize the club into a major force once more. Mercer was renowned for his tackling and perfectly timed interventions, and relished bringing the ball forward out of defence. He captained the club to the 1948 league title and the 1950 FA Cup – despite commuting from his home in Merseyside, where he ran a grocer's shop.

During the Second World War, along with a number of other top footballers of the time, Mercer accepted an invitation by the British Army to became a physical training instructor at Aldershot. In April 1954 he suffered a double fracture of his leg and was forced to retire from football. Initially he returned to his grocery business but was soon lured into management by Sheffield United. He went on to achieve significant success as boss of Manchester City, and also served as caretaker manager of England in 1974 after Sir Alf Ramsey's resignation.

FOOTBALL –STATS–

Joe Mercer

Name: Joseph Powell Mercer

Born: 1914

Died: 1990

Playing Career: 1932-1955

Clubs: Everton, Arsenal

Arsenal Appearances: 247

Goals: 2

England Appearances: 5

Managerial Career: Sheffield United, Aston Villa, Manchester City, Coventry City, England (caretaker)

> *The service of wonderful passes that flowed from this spindly bow-legged genius was, I am certain, 50 per cent of the reason for Arsenal's post-war successes.*
> Len Shackelton

Mercer with the FA Cup at Wembley, 1950.

FIR

Joe Mercer holds aloft the FA Cup trophy on the steps of Islington Town Hall as the team arrives for a civic reception, May 1950.

The Final Hurrah

The club's assault on the 1951/52 League Championship lasted, statistically at least, until the final game of the season against Manchester United at Old Trafford. But the odds were stacked almost impossibly against Arsenal, who needed to win by seven goals in order to secure the trophy. United routed them 6-1 to leave Arsenal with just the FA Cup to play for. The final against Newcastle gave Arsenal an opportunity to avenge their controversial defeat in 1932 – but it was not to be. Defender Walley Barnes picked up an early injury and, being in the days before substitutes, was rendered a passenger for the remainder of the game. To make matters worse, Arsenal suffered further injuries and by the end of the match they had only seven fit players on the pitch. With the numerical advantage, Newcastle won 1-0.

Tom Whittaker's side recovered to win the league title the following year but by the narrowest margin in history. Arsenal and Preston finished with identical records of 21 wins, 12 draws and nine defeats, and so goal average was needed to separate the sides. Arsenal's was 1.516, Preston's was 1.417. Arsenal took the honours by 0.099 of a goal. However, it was an ageing side and that dramatic title victory was to be its curtain call.

ABOVE Left to right: Swindin, Goring, Smith, Horsfield and Holton perform a synchronized exercise on the Highbury pitch.

BACKGROUND Queues of Arsenal fans outside Highbury hoping to get a ticket for the FA Cup semi-final against Chelsea, March 1952.

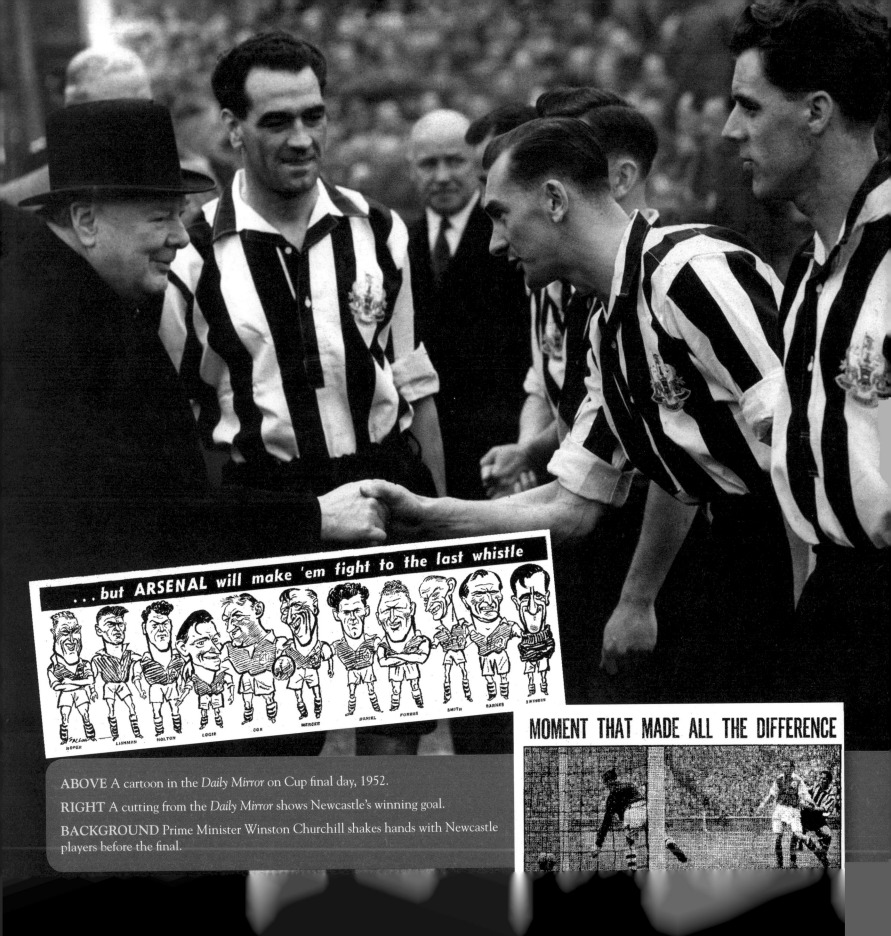

... but ARSENAL will make 'em fight to the last whistle

HOPER LISHMAN HOLTON LOGIE COX MERCER DANIEL FORBES SMITH BARNES SWINDIN

MOMENT THAT MADE ALL THE DIFFERENCE

ABOVE A cartoon in the *Daily Mirror* on Cup final day, 1952.

RIGHT A cutting from the *Daily Mirror* shows Newcastle's winning goal.

BACKGROUND Prime Minister Winston Churchill shakes hands with Newcastle players before the final.

ABOVE A boy is helped through the turnstiles at Highbury before a match against Blackpool, February 1953.

RIGHT Arsenal players Herd and Clapton challenge Leeds goalkeeper Wood during a league match at Highbury, September 1957.

Barnes holding the FA Cup in 1950.

60

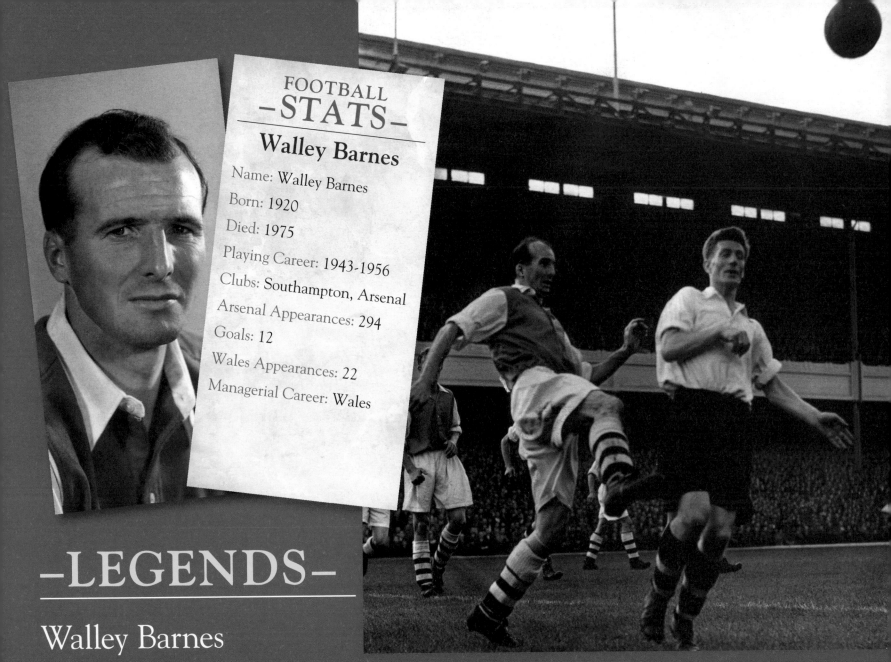

FOOTBALL -STATS-

Walley Barnes

Name: Walley Barnes

Born: 1920

Died: 1975

Playing Career: 1943-1956

Clubs: Southampton, Arsenal

Arsenal Appearances: 294

Goals: 12

Wales Appearances: 22

Managerial Career: Wales

-LEGENDS-

Walley Barnes

Walley Barnes's Arsenal career began away from the public glare of professional competition. After being spotted playing for Southampton as an inside-forward during the Second World War, he moved to London and played in virtually every position on the pitch for the remainder of the conflict. In 1944 he suffered a serious knee injury that doctors thought could force him to retire, but he defied their prognosis and returned to make his competitive debut in November 1946.

Barnes caught the eye with his assured performances at left-back. He was part of Arsenal's championship-winning side of 1947/48 and by this time had become a regular for Wales, winning his first cap against England in October 1947. Despite being given a torrid time by Stanley Matthews in a 3-0 defeat, the experience would not prevent Barnes becoming Wales captain.

In 1952, and now playing at right-back, Barnes was injured during the FA Cup final defeat to Newcastle and missed the entire following season. He later returned to the fold but was never the same player, and retired in 1956. During the last two years of his playing career, Barnes was also manager of the Welsh national team. After that, he entered broadcasting, and was one of the commentators for the first edition of *Match of the Day* in 1964.

LEFT Every club has its eccentric fans. Here is Arsenal supporter Mickey Renders, February 1953.

RIGHT Another dedicated supporter shows off her rosette and scarf, February 1953.

63

Jack Kelsey

Name: Alfred John Kelsey

Born: 1929

Died: 1992

Playing Career: 1949-1963

Clubs: Arsenal

Arsenal Appearances: 352

Wales Appearances: 41

-LEGENDS-

ABOVE Kelsey sees a shot wide during a match versus Newcastle at Highbury, November 1958.

Jack Kelsey

A former steelworker, Kelsey signed for Arsenal in 1949 from Winch Wen in the Swansea & District league, despite the club already boasting an established goalkeeper in George Swindin. After two years in the reserves, Kelsey finally made his first team debut against Charlton in February 1951, but a 5-2 defeat damaged his hopes of retaining his place and he made only three more appearances that season. Kelsey bided his time and eventually displaced his senior counterpart during the 1953/54 season.

Although his playing career coincided with a period of relative mediocrity for Arsenal, he is still regarded as one of the club's greatest ever goalkeepers. He was strong and agile, and in the days of the battering-ram centre-forward Kelsey's bravery narrowed the fear factor down to a straight battle of wills.

Kelsey also became a regular first choice keeper for Wales and was integral to their progress in the 1958 World Cup. They were knocked out 1-0 by eventual winners Brazil in the quarter-finals, with Kelsey left with the "honour" of being beaten by Pelé's first ever goal for Brazil. "I think this kid has got a good future," Kelsey commented about the 17-year-old after the game.

The club's success waned in the 1950s, with Tom Whittaker unable to attract any major stars. The strain took its toll, and Whittaker died of a heart attack in 1956, aged 58. After his death, the club tried to replicate the initial success they had achieved with Whittaker through hiring from within, by giving the job to two former players – Jack Crayston (as caretaker) and George Swindin. But neither could rekindle the club's former glories.

JACK CRAYSTON

LAST RESPECTS

Arsenal Stadium is closed this morning for the first Monday since the war.

This is to enable every member of the playing, office and ground staffs to pay their last respects at the funeral of secretary-manager Tom Whittaker, who died last Wednesday.

RIGHT Jack Crayston, assistant coach under Tom Whittaker and caretaker manager after Whittaker's death.

HE WAS ARSENAL...

By TONY HORSTEAD

THE entire Soccer world was saddened yesterday by the news of the death of one of its best-loved characters — Tom Whittaker, secretary-manager of Arsenal.

Burly Tom, the strong man with the gentle touch, will be sincerely mourned by all who came in touch with him in any capacity.

Courtesy was the keynote of this great man's character. Naturally courteous himself, he demanded it from all his staff.

He was a strict disciplinarian, but he never found it necessary to raise his voice.

Although Tom, who was fifty-nine, had been ill for several months and forced to take a rest from High-bury, he still kept in touch right to the end.

Before assistant manager Jack Crayston announced his team each week, he discussed it with Tom by telephone.

Tom was born in Aldershot, but spent most of his childhood in Newcastle. He joined Arsenal as a centre forward in 1919 and became a half back.

His playing career ended after he smashed a knee-cap while touring Australia with the F.A. in 1925.

It was then that Herbert Chapman persuaded him to join the training staff, and Tom's treatment room at Highbury became world famous. Stars of almost every sport went to him for help.

During the war he rose to Squadron-Leader in the engineering branch of the RAF and was awarded the M.B.E.

He succeeded George Allison in 1947, and then took Arsenal twice to the League championship, and twice to the F.A. Cup Final.

In Amsterdam tears ran down the face of Ted Drake, Chelsea's manager, when he heard the news.

"He will be missed wherever football is played because Tom was known and loved all over the world," he said.

And 30,000 Dutchmen bore him out as they stood in silence before the match between the Football Combination and a Dutch eleven.

TOM WHITTAKER

–LEGENDS–

Tom Whittaker

Whittaker spent his early football career in the northeast of England as a youth player, whilst training as a marine engineer. After serving in the Royal Navy during the First World War, he joined Leslie Knighton's Arsenal in November 1919. He first played as centre-forward then as wing-half. In 1925, during a tour of Australia, he broke his kneecap and was forced to retire. Resolving to remain in football, he joined Arsenal's coaching staff and studied physiotherapy. He became the club's first team trainer in 1927, whilst still younger than many of the players on the pitch, and played an important role in reforming the training and physiotherapy regime at the club.

After Herbert Chapman's death, Whittaker continued to serve under his successor, George Allison, and also became a trainer for the England national team. During the Second World War, Whittaker served as a pilot in the Royal Air Force, achieving the rank of squadron leader, and was awarded an MBE for his contribution to the D-Day missions. At the end of the war, Whittaker resumed his role as trainer at Arsenal. After Allison's retirement in 1947, he became the club's new manager, winning the league twice and the FA Cup. However, the club's fortunes wavered in the 1950s, and, perhaps through stresses of the job, he died of a heart attack in 1956.

FOOTBALL –STATS–

Tom Whittaker

Name: Thomas James Whittaker

Born: 1898

Died: 1956

Playing Career: 1919-1925

Clubs: Arsenal

Arsenal Appearances: 70

Goals: 2

Managerial Career: Arsenal

ABOVE Physiotherapist Bertie Mee watches over a player during a resistance training exercise.

FAR LEFT Tommy Docherty, who played for Arsenal between 1958 and 1961.

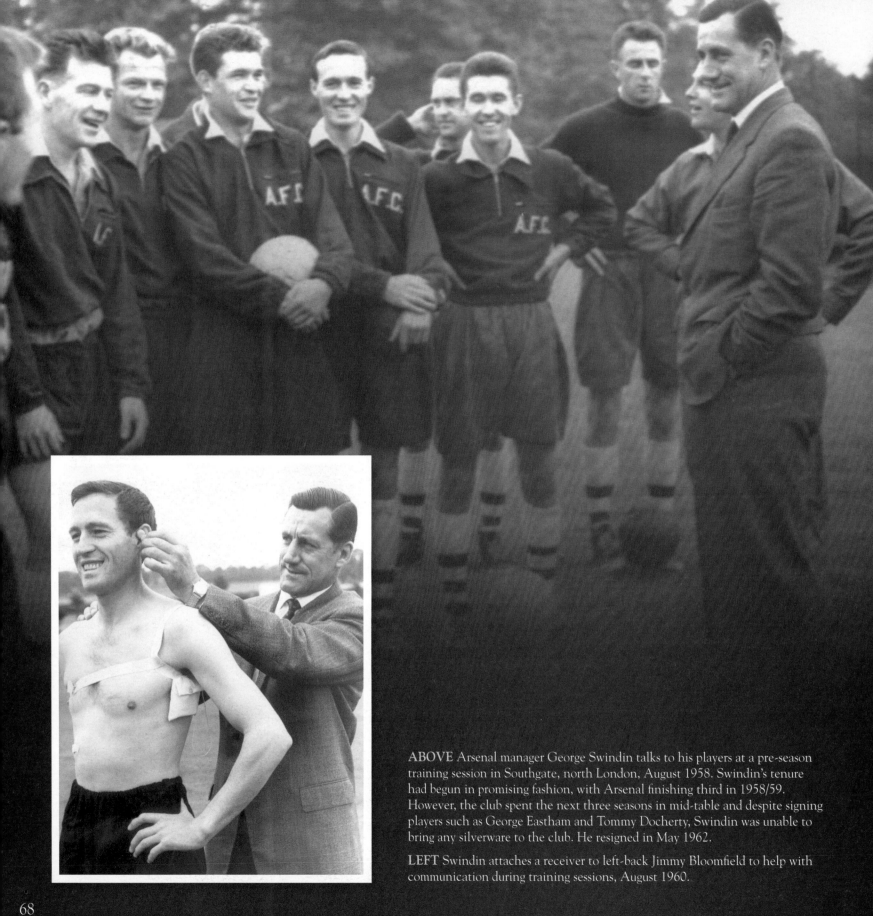

ABOVE Arsenal manager George Swindin talks to his players at a pre-season training session in Southgate, north London, August 1958. Swindin's tenure had begun in promising fashion, with Arsenal finishing third in 1958/59. However, the club spent the next three seasons in mid-table and despite signing players such as George Eastham and Tommy Docherty, Swindin was unable to bring any silverware to the club. He resigned in May 1962.

LEFT Swindin attaches a receiver to left-back Jimmy Bloomfield to help with communication during training sessions, August 1960.

REVIE FOR ARSENAL ?

SWINDIN GETS ANGRY

Paper Talk

Paper Talk
The short-lived Swindin era seemed to coincide with a time when media hyperbole moved into overdrive. Sensationalist stories and transfer tittle-tattle were the order of the day, and Swindin found himself on the receiving end of some provocative headlines.

Arsenal Bombshell

SWINDIN TO SELL 7 MORE !

By KEN JONES

ARSENAL manager George Swindin dropped a bombshell yesterday by slapping a "for sale" notice on SEVEN of his players.

These are the men listed in a circular sent to other League clubs: Jim Fotheringham (centre half), Cliff Holton (wing half or centre forward), Mike Tiddy (outside left), Con Sullivan (goalkeeper), Don Bennett (full back), Peter Davies (wing half), and Ray

● These are six of the men Arsenal no longer want (left to right): Jim Fotheringham, Cliff Holton, Mike Tiddy, Con Sullivan, Don Bennett, Ray Dixon.

ARSENAL recaptured the title of Britain's "Bank of England" club yesterday when they paid £35,000 for Wolves' tough tackling wing half Eddie Clamp.

Manager George Swindin has wanted Clamp for many months, and when Wolves boss Stan Cullis phoned yesterday to say Clamp was for sale, Swindin dashed to Wolverhampton and completed the deal.

The Bank of England Club
Arsenal's dominance in the 1930s transformed them into the richest club in the world and their extravagance in the transfer market led to them being dubbed the "Bank of England Club", as referenced in this *Daily Mirror* cutting from 1961.

Manager Swindin is quitting Highbury at end of the season—'Things just didn't go his way,' says chairman

The Wright Man?

When Billy Wright was appointed Arsenal manager in 1962, replacing George Swindin, his reputation was based entirely on his illustrious playing career as captain of Wolves and England. His managerial experience was negligible, and his only association with Arsenal was that he had been a fan of the club as a boy. It seemed a major gamble to give the job to this highly respected, but unproven, outsider.

ABOVE Billy Wright stands outside the entrance to Highbury's Marble Halls, 1963.

LEFT Wright with his wife, the singer Joy Beverley of the Beverley Sisters, and their daughter Victoria. Thanks to his famous partner Wright became a media personality, years before the cult of celebrity permeated football.

–LEGENDS–

Joe Baker

Liverpool-born Baker made his name with Scottish club Hibernian, before moving to Torino of Italy in 1961. However, he was uncomfortable with the level of press intrusion and spent much of his time cooped up with Scotland's Denis Law in their Turin apartment. On one of his occasional forays outside, he knocked a photographer into a canal. Baker was also involved in a serious car crash whilst in Italy, leaving him requiring life-saving surgery.

He returned to the UK in July 1962, joining Billy Wright's Arsenal for a club record £70,000. He made his debut a month later, and in all spent four seasons at Highbury, becoming one of the club's most prolific goalscorers of all time. Despite his goals, Arsenal finished no higher than seventh during Baker's time at the club. He was sold to Nottingham Forest in 1966.

Although he was eligible to play for Scotland, he made his England debut in 1959, making him the first player to represent England without having ever played for an English club. In all he won eight caps, narrowly missing the cut for the 1966 World Cup squad. After retiring from football, Baker ran a pub and worked for Hibernian's hospitality service. He died aged 63.

Billy Wright gives his new signing a private tour of Highbury.

FOOTBALL –STATS–

Joe Baker

Name: Joseph Henry Baker

Born: 1940

Died: 2003

Playing Career: 1957-1974

Clubs: Torino, Arsenal, Nottingham Forest, Sunderland, Hibernian, Raith Rovers

Arsenal Appearances: 156

Goals: 100

England Appearances: 8

Goals: 3

Managerial Career: Albion Rovers

BELOW Baker signs for Arsenal, watched by legendary Italian football agent, Gigi Peronace (left) and Billy Wright, July 1962.

71

ABOVE Arsenal goalkeeper Jim Furnell jumps for a high ball with Manchester United's Bobby Charlton at Old Trafford, February 1964.

LEFT Furnell is beaten by Liverpool's Roger Hunt during a league match at Anfield, August 1964. The game was the first to be broadcast on *Match of the Day*.

BELOW Arsenal's 1965-66 squad.

—LEGENDS—

George Eastham

George Eastham's influence on football extended far beyond the hallowed turf, where his magical left foot and intricate passing made him one of the most gifted players of his generation. Hailing from an eminent football family, his gravitas within the game helped bring about a landmark ruling that began a shift in the balance of power from clubs to players. When his employers Newcastle United refused to grant him a transfer at the end of his contract in 1959, Eastham went on strike for eight months. Eventually Newcastle relented, allowing him to move to Arsenal, but Eastham continued his crusade and took his former club to the High Court. The British transfer system was judged to be unreasonable and reforms were introduced, giving more freedom to players wanting to move clubs.

Eastham's time at Arsenal was often turbulent: as well as the court case against Newcastle, he fell out with the club over wages and asked for a transfer after losing his place to Joe Baker in 1962. He eventually came off the transfer list and returned to the side, but in 1966 he was sold to Stoke City, where he would later manage. In 1978, he emigrated to South Africa and set up his own sportswear business as well as serving as a children's football coach.

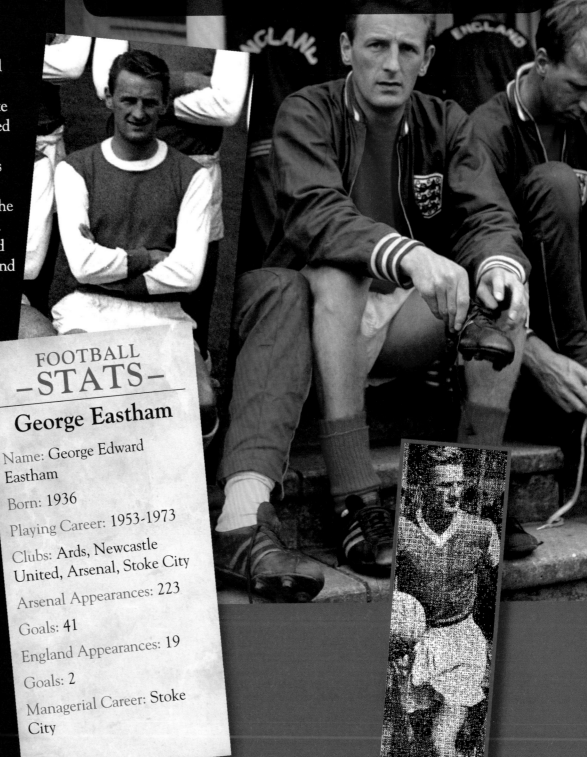

George Eastham after an England training session, circa 1964. Eastham was the only Arsenal player in England's 1966 World Cup-winning squad, But in Alf Ramsey's workmanlike England team there was no room for both him and Bobby Charlton to show their flair, and he didn't play a single minute of the tournament.

FOOTBALL —STATS—

George Eastham

Name: George Edward Eastham

Born: 1936

Playing Career: 1953-1973

Clubs: Ards, Newcastle United, Arsenal, Stoke City

Arsenal Appearances: 223

Goals: 41

England Appearances: 19

Goals: 2

Managerial Career: Stoke City

—AND ONLY 4,554 AT HIGHBURY TO SEE ARSENAL THRASHED

Arsenal started strongly under Billy Wright, finishing seventh in 1962/63 and qualifying for Europe for the first time in the club's history. But managers of top clubs have always been judged on trophies, and on that score Wright fell short. Highbury attendances were down and after a poor 1965/66 season the writing was on the wall. Wright was dismissed in the summer of 1966.

Despite his apparent failure, a theory abounds that he laid the foundations for the success that would soon follow. In 1966 the club's youth team, boasting the likes of Charlie George, John Radford, Pat Rice and Ray Kennedy, all of whom had been carefully nurtured by Wright, won the FA Youth Cup. The seeds were sown.

SIDE TWO

To: BILLY WRIGHT
From: LOYAL ARSENAL SUPPORTERS

6th APRIL 1963

WE* PROTEST MOST STRONGLY AT WAY IN WHICH ARSENAL HAVE BLINDLY REFUSED TO BUY NEW PLAYERS TO STRENGTHEN A SIDE THAT IS A DISGRACE TO THE NAME OF A GREAT CLUB.
WE* DEMAND THAT SOME OF ARSENAL'S ENORMOUS WEALTH IS INVESTED IN NEW PLAYERS TO ENSURE THAT THE GUNNERS WILL ONCE AGAIN SOON EMERGE AS THE GREATEST CLUB IN THE COUNTRY

UP THE GUNNERS!
* NAMES OVERLEAF

A letter and petition to Billy Wright from fans demanding that new players are purchased, April 1963.

ONLY 8,738 (LOWEST LEAGUE GATE) SINCE THE WAR AT ARSENAL

"My youngsters had just won the FA Youth Cup. I am convinced I was on the verge of a breakthrough.
Billy Wright

> *Billy Wright had neither the guile nor the authority to make things work and he reacted almost childishly to criticism.*
>
> Brian Glanville

Billy Wright's wife says: Arsenal sacked him—I'm furious

By PAULA JAMES

BLONDE Joy Beverley wiped angry tears from her eyes last night and said: "My husband never resigned—he was fired. And I'm furious."

Joy, eldest of the famous singing Beverley sisters, is the wife of Billy Wright—who figured in a Soccer sensation yesterday when it was announced that he has resigned his £3,500-a-year plus job as manager of the Arsenal club.

Wright himself said that, on his return from a holiday in Italy, he was "invited to resign" by Arsenal chairman Denis Hill-Wood.

"He told me the directors are worried by the club's lack of success," Wright added. "It was felt a change of manager would be the best thing."

Joy said at their home in Lyonsdown-road, Barnet: "It's been the most dreadful shock.

Joy—"It's a shock."

'WE BOTH WEPT . .'

Billy came home this afternoon, put his arms round me and suggested we should have a night out together.

"I knew immediately something was wrong, and then he told me what had happened.

"I burst into tears—and then he cried, too. We both just sat there weeping. It's the most heartbreaking thing that has ever happened to us."

Holiday

Joy and Billy — they have been married for eight years—got home from their twelve-day holiday in Italy on Sunday night.

"And a fine homecoming this has been," said Joy as she picked up her 20-month-old younger daughter, Babette, and hugged her.

"Billy is a wonderful man, a good man and a trier," she went on. "He just isn't the resigning type.

"I don't care what he says—I know they told him to go and I don't see the point in being hypocritical about it."

Joy went on: "The worst thing is I cannot be a comfort to Billy because I am annoyed with him for refusing to admit he was fired.

"I don't see why he should cover up for the people who pushed him out."

Then Joy wiped away a tear and said:

"Anyway, if Billy is no longer manager of Arsenal, one thing is sure —he'll live longer."

Wright says "I feel sorry for the chairman"—See Page 27.

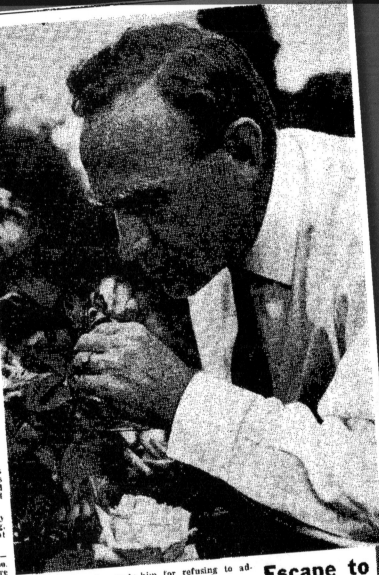

Escape to his roses

Billy Wright, centre of a Soccer sensation, is pictured last night relaxing among the roses in his garden.

75

BERTIE'S BOYS SHOW 'BRITISH IS BEST'

A GAME rich in skill and explosive endeavour left the fans of Arsenal and West Ham, last night, with much to remember and a lot to look forward to.

This should be a season worth watching for all of them.

Full of fitness and fire, Arsenal, in the end, had to survive the sort of onslaught that would have shattered any side from their immediate past.

West Ham, forced to pull back from two goals down, discovered the resolution that has too often been missing from their game. It all proved a lot and promised much.

This all-London clash—Arsenal's first home match under Bertie Mee's management — pulled in

By KEN JONES   Arsenal 2, W. Ham 1

40,533 fans, 10,000 more than for Highbury's opening home game last year.

With Geoff Hurst, Johnny Byrne, Peter Brabrook and John Sissons all going in and going close in a tremendous second-half, Arsenal had luck to back their bravery and West Ham none to back their skill.

West Ham were worth a point and their football is obviously a season or so ahead of the stuff that a revitalised Arsenal will offer in the months to come.

But as West Ham's football flowed and Arsenal met it with a barrier of red shirts that hurled and dived at the ball, this became the best of the British brand of the game.

One move, so incisive and swift it was over almost before it began, left Arsenal without answer to the skill of Byrne and Hurst and it was only the foot of a post that robbed Hurst of an equaliser.

Arsenal began by running hard and hurling centres at a suspect goalkeeper, Jim Standen.

It paid off after only four minutes, when a cross from left winger George Armstrong was pushed on to the underside of the bar by John Radford for Tommy Baldwin to finish off.

Challenge

Arsenal went further in front in the thirty-seventh minute.

A long ball from left back Peter Storey left Radford and Standen challenging in mid-air and the ball went through from both of them and into the net.

Beaten by the brilliance

of goalkeeper Bonetti against Chelsea on Saturday, West Ham had now to prove they could come from behind.

A brave goal by Byrne—a header and then a shot them back into the match and it was the signal for them to strike true form.

Arsenal were running out of stamina, and failing to win the ball or keep it in mid-field.

It was a credit to their defensive determination that they survived.

It seemed inevitable that West Ham must score, must equalise — and perhaps win.

They didn't, and probably they are still wondering why.

After the sacking of Billy Wright, Arsenal, without a trophy since 1953, were in the doldrums. The club's previous attempts at promoting from within had proved unsuccessful, but undeterred the board opted to do the same again – though this time with a twist: the club's physiotherapist Bertie Mee was offered the job. Mee, who had began his career as a footballer, accepted, but asked for a get-out clause that would allow him to return to his old role if things didn't work out.

Mee recruited the more experienced and tactically astute Dave Sexton and Don Howe as his assistants, allowing him to focus on instilling renewed discipline at the club and remoulding the side in his image. He wheeled and dealed on the transfer market, bringing in the likes of defender Bob McNab and forward George Graham, and blooding talented youngsters such as strikers Charlie George and Ray Kennedy. New standards were set, and the dawn of a more fruitful era had arrived.

OPPOSITE George Graham, one of Bertie Mee's first signings as Arsenal boss.

TOP George Best, Pat Crerand, Frank McLintock and John Radford rise majestically during a match between Manchester United and Arsenal at Old Trafford, October 1967.

RIGHT Manchester United's Denis Law and Arsenal's Ian Ure square up during an incident which led to them both being sent off.

BELOW A groundsman sweeps the goal-line clear of snow during a match between Arsenal and Sheffield Wednesday at Highbury, December 1967. The game was abandoned after 47 minutes.

OPPOSITE Arsenal manager Bertie Mee on the Highbury pitch, July 1967.

The Fickle Game

1968-1985

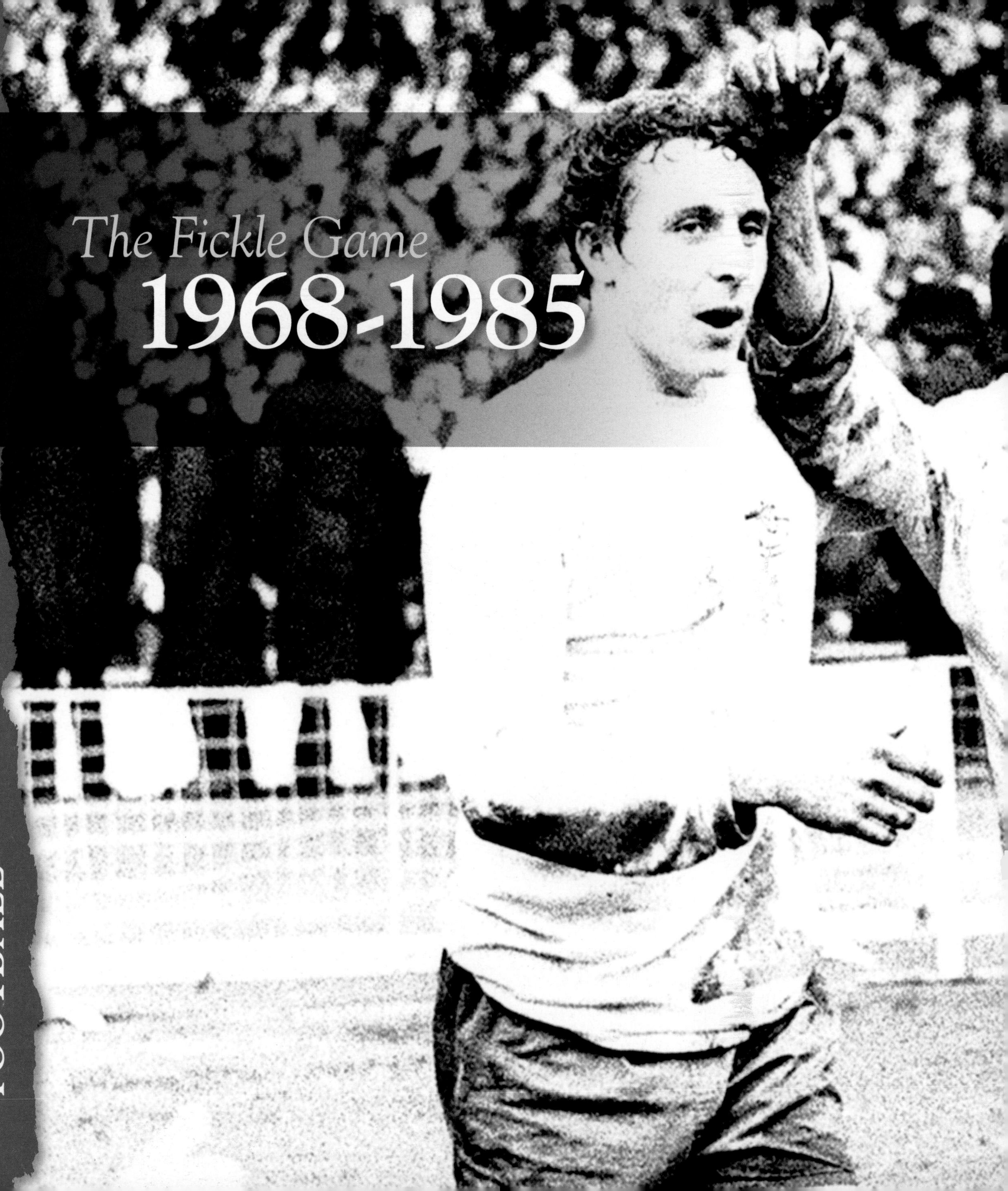

John Radford (left) and a distraught Bobby Gould after losing to Swindon Town in the League Cup final at Wembley, March 1969.

1968 Arsenal lose the League Cup final to Leeds. 1969 Arsenal lose the League Cup final to Swindon. 1970 Arsenal win the Fairs Cup against Anderlecht. 1971 Arsenal win the League and FA Cup Double for the first time. 1972 Arsenal play in the European Cup for the first time. 1973 Ken Friar is appointed club secretary. 1976 Bertie Mee resigns as manager and is replaced by Terry Neill. 1978 Arsenal lose the FA Cup final to Ipswich. 1979 Arsenal win the FA Cup against Manchester United. 1980 Arsenal lose two Cup finals in the same season – the FA Cup to West Ham and the European Cup Winners' Cup to Valencia. 1982 Peter Hill-Wood is appointed chairman following the death of his father, Denis. 1983 David Dein is appointed as a club director. 1983 Terry Neill is sacked as manager and is replaced by Don Howe.

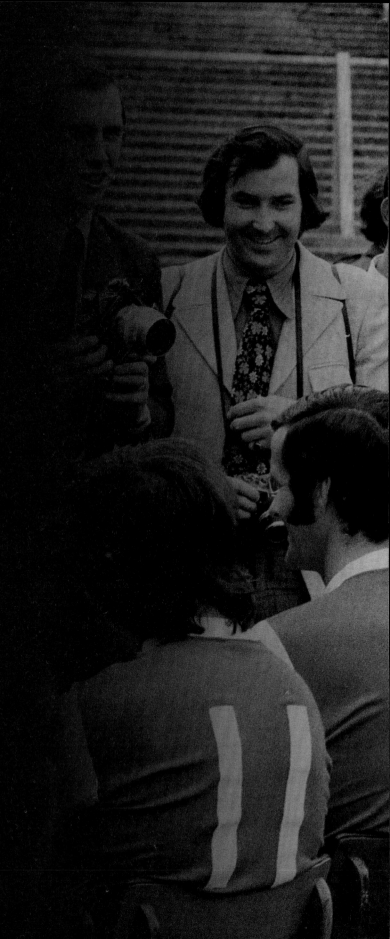

Frank McLintock waves during a press photoshoot, 1971.

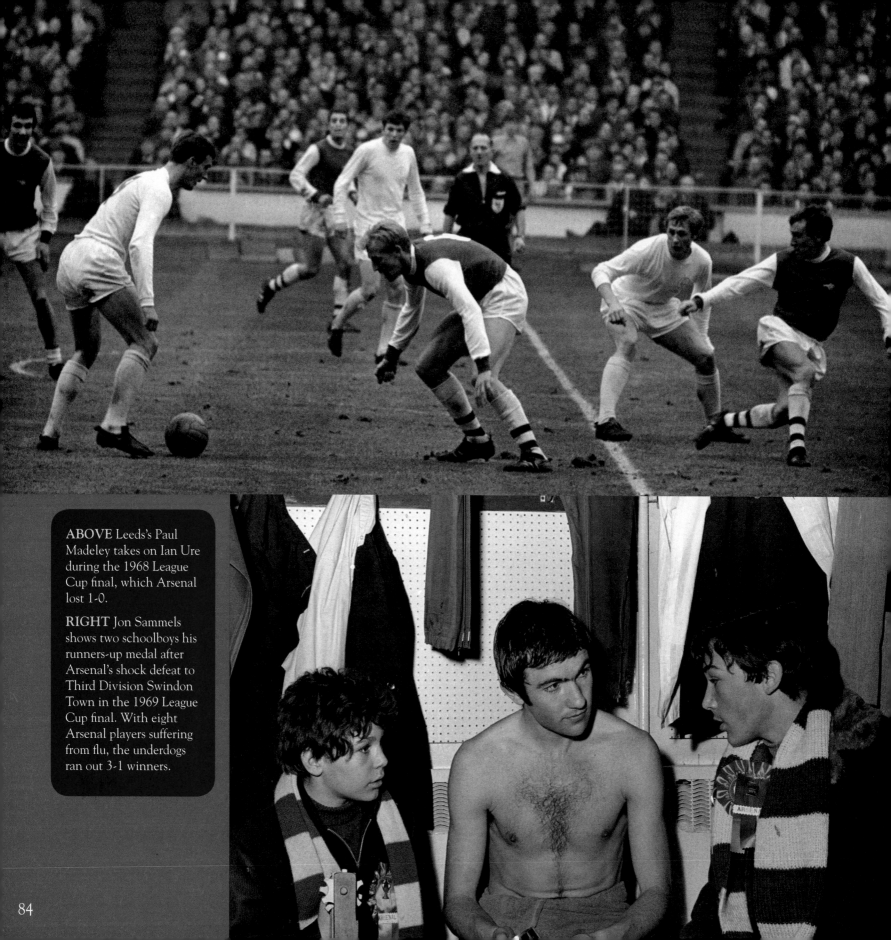

ABOVE Leeds's Paul Madeley takes on Ian Ure during the 1968 League Cup final, which Arsenal lost 1-0.

RIGHT Jon Sammels shows two schoolboys his runners-up medal after Arsenal's shock defeat to Third Division Swindon Town in the 1969 League Cup final. With eight Arsenal players suffering from flu, the underdogs ran out 3-1 winners.

ABOVE Ian Ure inspecting the Highbury pitch, January 1968. After signing for the club in 1963, Ure developed a reputation for being error-prone, characterized by his performance against Swindon at Wembley when his mistake led to the first goal. Despite his perceived limitations, he made 202 appearances for Arsenal.

LEFT Arsenal Back Room girls stroking the club's feline mascot "Gunner" on the eve of the League Cup final, March 1969.

86

OPPOSITE A referee from Finsbury Park stands outside High

ABOVE Pat Rice serves a customer in a greengrocers on Gill
Highbury, February 1968. He continued to work in the store
professional with Arsenal in 1966.

Arsenal players turn to view the result of a Derby County free kick during a league match at Highbury, November 1969.

ABOVE Coach Don Howe, February 1969.

OPPOSITE Terry Neill with his bride Sandra after their wedding ceremony in his home town of Bangor, County Down, November 1969.

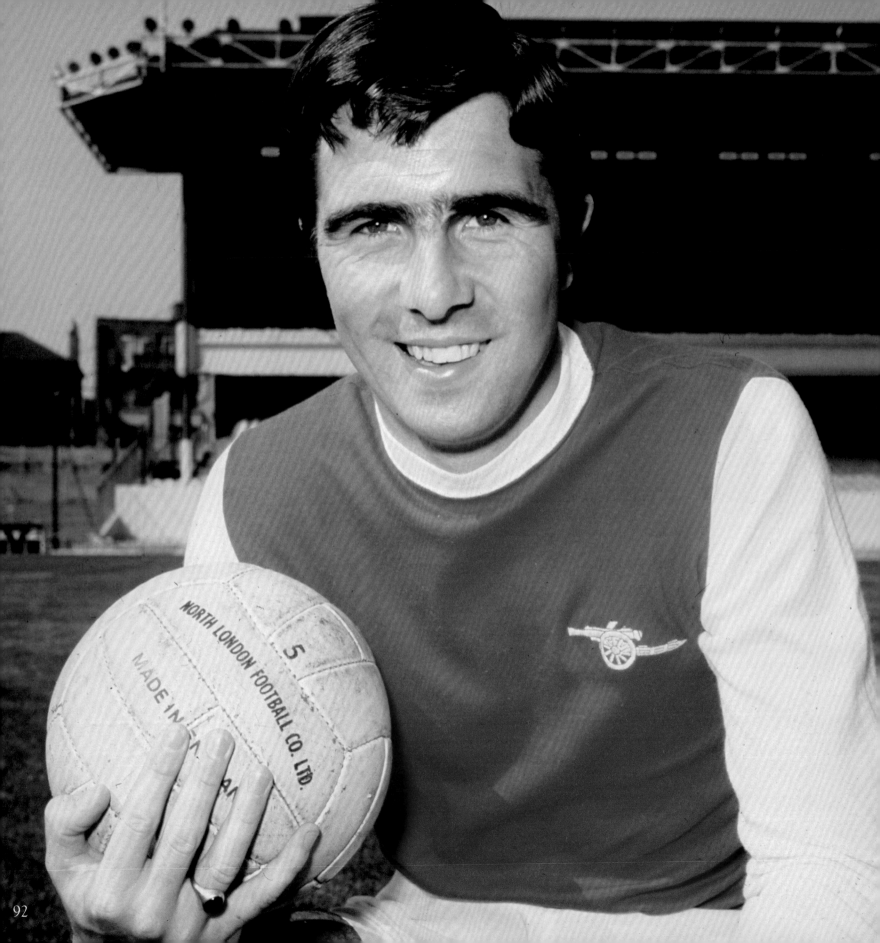

LEFT Jon Sammels rearranging his footwear after losing a boot in a game against Manchester City, December 1969.

BELOW George Graham makes an acrobatic clearance in a game against Blackpool, November 1970.

OPPOSITE Bobby Gould, who played for Arsenal between 1968 and 1970.

ABOVE Peter Marinello puts pen to paper on his move to Arsenal from Scottish club Hibernian with manager Bertie Mee looking on, January 1970. The Scot had been dubbed "the next George Best" – not only for his ability on the pitch, but also his good looks and night life exploits.

TOP RIGHT Giving an autograph to a young fan on the steps of the Marble Halls after signing for the club.

RIGHT Marinello in action.

OPPOSITE Tending to his hair as his colleagues prepare for an FA Cup game against Blackpool, January 1970.

> "It was all about win or lose, have a good time."
>
> Peter Marinello

ABOVE Jon Sammels and Charlie George celebrate after Sammels's goal against Ajax in the Fairs Cup semi-final at Highbury, April 1970.

RIGHT Frank McLintock is carried off the Highbury pitch holding the Fairs Cup.

OPPOSITE An emotional McLintock embraces team-mate Eddie Kelly.

After 17 years without a trophy, Arsenal went into the 1969/70 season in hope more than expectation. The Inter-Cities Fairs Cup pitted them against relative cannon fodder, and their progression included a nine-goal route of Dinamo Bacau over two legs. The semi-finals, however, saw them face Ajax – a team boasting the likes of Johan Cruyff, Rudi Krol and Piet Keizer. The Dutch giants were disposed of, leaving only Anderlecht between Arsenal and an end to their trophy drought.

The first leg was a near disaster, with Arsenal 3-0 down before a late goal by Ray Kennedy gave them a lifeline. Six days later at Highbury, Eddie Kelly's early goal settled the nerves before John Radford squared the tie on aggregate. Jon Sammels made it 3-0 and the final whistle saw Arsenal fans pour on to the pitch to celebrate. After waiting so long for success, it would have taken a heart of stone to condemn them.

> *That was probably the greatest emotional moment of my life.*
> Bertie Mee

Ray Kennedy heads over the on-rushing Beveren goalkeeper during a Fairs Cup tie at Highbury, December 1970. Arsenal won 4-0 on the night, and on aggregate, but were prevented from retaining their crown by FC Cologne, who beat them in the following round, thus also denying the club the chance of winning the Treble.

BELOW John Radford celebrates a goal during a league match against West Ham at Highbury, January 1971. Radford scored 149 goals for the club and was also highly regarded for his work ethic and selfless contribution to the team.

OPPOSITE Charlie George, Frank McLintock and team-mates.

The lads were all hugging each other as though we'd scored. But I was the one who had to stick it in. And past Gordon Banks too!

Peter Storey

BELOW A goalmouth scramble during Arsenal's dramatic 2-2 draw with Stoke City in the FA Cup semi-final at Hillsborough, March 1971. Arsenal were 2-0 down at half-time before two goals from Peter Storey brought them back into the tie. The equalizer came in injury time from the penalty spot. As Storey stepped up to face Gordon Banks, Bob Wilson sank to his knees at the other end and looked to the heavens. His prayers were answered and Arsenal were back in the hunt for the fabled Double.

LEFT Peter Storey is congratulated by a fan on the pitch after the game.

TOP Jack Charlton scores a controversial last-minute goal for Leeds as Arsenal players appeal for offside, April 1971. With Leeds their closest rivals, the defeat left Arsenal's title hopes in the balance with just two matches left to play.

BELOW Furious Arsenal players, led by normally mild-mannered goalkeeper Bob Wilson, protest to the referee.

103

The 1970/71 league season came down to the final game with Arsenal trailing Leeds by just one point. Arsenal's last fixture was against, of all teams, Tottenham at White Hart Lane. The gates were locked more than an hour before kick-off with well over 50,000 spectators inside. Twice that number were left outside, with the traffic in the area so congested that the match referee was forced to abandon his car and fight his way on foot through the crowds.

On the pitch, the permutations were as follows: a victory or goalless draw would be good enough for Arsenal, but a defeat or score-draw would see the title go up north. At 0-0 with three minutes left, Arsenal were on course, but with Spurs pushing for a vital win in their chase for European qualification, the Gunners took advantage. George Armstrong crossed and Ray Kennedy headed home. When the whistle blew, thousands of fans raced on to the pitch. Arsenal had won their eighth league championship, making them England's most decorated club at the time. And, crucially, the first part of the Double had been secured.

> *Arsenal have got as much chance of being handed the title by Spurs as I have of being given the Crown Jewels.*
>
> Alan Mullery

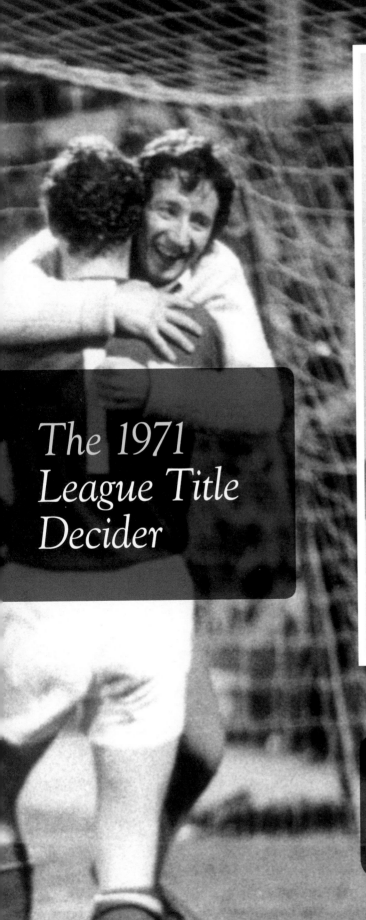

The 1971 League Title Decider

OPPOSITE TOP Arsenal players celebrate after Ray Kennedy's header, the goal that won them the league championship, May 1971.

OPPOSITE BOTTOM Arsenal fans smother the White Hart Lane pitch.

LEFT A fan hugs Bob Wilson after the final whistle.

ABOVE Frank McLintock and Bertie Mee share a tender moment after victory.

Young Arsenal fans on Blundell Street, Islington, ahead of the FA Cup final against Liverpool, May 1971.

The 1971 FA Cup Final

The Cup final proved to be a battle of tactical fortitude with neither team able to produce a goal in regular time. Liverpool finally made the breakthrough two minutes into extra time, when Steve Heighway caught out Bob Wilson to score inside his near post.

Wilson's rare blunder was quickly forgotten as substitute Eddie Kelly levelled for Arsenal nine minutes later, though Graham also claimed the goal as he took a swing at the ball which deceived Ray Clemence. A draw looked odds-on, but with eight minutes left a visibly drained Charlie George found one last burst of energy, letting fly with a 20-yard shot which gave Clemence no chance. George "celebrated" by laying on the ground, arms and legs extended. He had earned his breather – and Arsenal had earned their Double.

ABOVE LEFT The Duke of Kent is introduced to Mee during the pre-match meet-and-greet at Wembley, May 1971.

ABOVE LEFT Bertie Mee leads his team out at Wembley.

BACKGROUND Peter Storey battles for the ball.

BELOW Charlie George lies on his back with his hands in the air after scoring the winning goal at Wembley. This would become one of the FA Cup's most iconic images.

ABOVE George conforms to tradition in the post-match celebrations.

Victorious skipper Frank McLintock is hoisted aloft by team-mates. McLintock was at his inspirational best in the final; with three Wembley runners-up medals he refused to be beaten.

> "I wanted to win the cup for Frank McLintock. The league championship was for my chairman Denis Hill-Wood. For myself? I wouldn't mind the European Cup next season."
>
> Bertie Mee

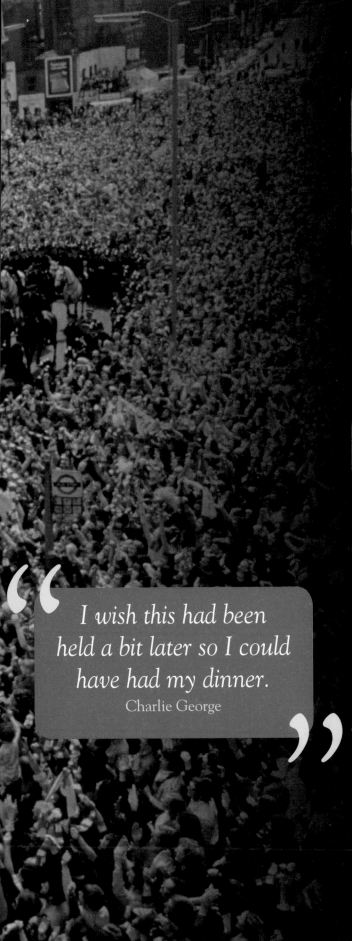

> *I wish this had been held a bit later so I could have had my dinner.*
> Charlie George

LEFT The Arsenal squad arrives at Islington Town Hall during the open-top bus parade to celebrate the Double.

ABOVE Joyful fans after the FA Cup final victory against Liverpool.

–LEGENDS–

Charlie George

The original cockney rebel, Charlie George was not just an Arsenal legend but an icon of the Seventies. Born in Islington, George had watched Arsenal from the stands as a boy, and this contributed to his cult status as a player. He was also blessed with natural ability and was renowned for his powerful shooting. He made his first-team debut in August 1969 and became a regular in the side that season. He played a significant role in Arsenal's Double triumph, including the winning goal in the FA Cup final, followed by his famous prostrate celebration.

   George played four more seasons at Highbury, but was increasingly hampered by injuries and also an unruly streak that didn't sit well with disciplinarian Bertie Mee. In 1972 he was in trouble for headbutting Liverpool's Kevin Keegan. By Christmas 1974 he had been transfer listed, and he moved to Derby County in July 1975. Here he achieved moderate success, winning his solitary England cap during his spell at the club, before moving to the United States to play for NASL club Minnesota Kicks. Following his retirement he continued to attend Arsenal matches as a supporter, and retains strong connections with the club to this day.

FOOTBALL
–STATS–

Charlie George

Name: Frederick Charles George

Born: 1950

Playing Career: 1968-1983

Clubs: Arsenal, Derby County, Minnesota Kicks, Southampton, Bulova, Bournemouth, Derby County, Dundee United

Arsenal Appearances: 179

Goals: 49

England Appearances: 1

OPPOSITE The King of Highbury, May 1972.

TOP LEFT George on guitar, Graham on drums, at the team party to celebrate the 1971 Double.

TOP RIGHT Outside his house leaning on his Rolls-Royce car, September 1975.

ABOVE In a men's clothing store looking for Christmas bargains.

–LEGENDS–

Frank McLintock

Frank McLintock's on-pitch demeanour commanded respect and enabled him to drag his team out of the doldrums when all seemed lost. He started his career as a wing-half at Leicester City, before moving to Arsenal in 1964. He spent the next nine seasons at Highbury, moving from midfield to centre-half due to an injury crisis. He thrived in his new role, demonstrating an outstanding reading of the game coupled with a new-found positional discipline, and in 1967 earned the club captaincy.

After the League Cup final defeats of 1968 and 1969, however, McLintock became so disheartened he handed in a transfer request. Manager Bertie Mee persuaded him to stay, and he went on to win three major trophies in two years – the Fairs Cup and the League and FA Cup Double. McLintock ended the 1971 campaign as Footballer of the Year, and an MBE followed a year later. He finally left the club in 1973, with his name firmly etched in Arsenal folklore. After moving to Queens Park Rangers, he retired from playing in 1977, before going into management at Leicester and Brentford.

FOOTBALL –STATS–

Frank McLintock

Name: Frank McLintock George

Born: 1939

Playing Career: 1957-1977

Clubs: Leicester City, Arsenal, Queens Park Rangers

Arsenal Appearances: 403

Goals: 32

Scotland Appearances: 9

Goals: 1

Managerial Career: Leicester City, Brentford

LEFT Holding the FA Cup trophy aloft in 1971.

OPPOSITE TOP Going head-to-head with novelist Jackie Collins for a promotional shoot, February 1979.

OPPOSITE BOTTOM Helped off the pitch holding the Fairs Cup, April 1970.

> " *Just going into the ground or the dressing room at Highbury was very grand, it was like going to a lovely hotel. You almost felt like royalty going there.* "
> Frank McLintock

TOP LEFT Television pundit Jimmy Hill running the line during a league match between Arsenal and Liverpool at Highbury, September 1972. During the game, linesman Dennis Drewitt pulled a muscle and was unable to continue. The matchday announcer put a message over the loudspeaker asking if anyone was a qualified referee. Hill, who was at Highbury as a spectator, came out of the crowd, donned a tracksuit and saved the day. The match finished 0-0.

ABOVE The 1971/72 Arsenal squad.

TOP RIGHT One absentee from the squad photo is Alan Ball, who signed for Arsenal from Everton in the middle of the 1971/72 season. Here he is taking one last walk around the Goodison Park pitch after completing his Highbury move.

FOOTBALL
–STATS–

Alan Ball

Name: Alan James Ball, Jr

Born: 1945

Died: 2007

Playing Career: 1962-1984

Clubs: Blackpool, Everton, Arsenal, Southampton, Philadelphia Fury, Vancouver Whitecaps, Blackpool, Southampton, Eastern AA, Bristol Rovers

Arsenal Appearances: 217

Goals: 52

England Appearances: 72

Goals: 8

Managerial Career: Blackpool, Portsmouth, Stoke City, Exeter City, Southampton, Manchester City, Portsmouth

Alan Ball

A 1966 World Cup-winner, Alan Ball's arrival at Highbury in December 1971 for a British record fee of £220,000 lent a touch of flair to a side considered functional but effective. The former Everton player's technique and passing ability, illuminated by his trademark white boots, quickly made him an influential player in the post-Double Arsenal side. However, he was unable to land any silverware with the club.

At the start of the 1973/74 season he took on the club captaincy. Injury ruled him out of the start of the following campaign, and results suffered in his absence. Relegation was averted but Ball lasted just one more full season at Highbury, helping the struggling side secure their top-flight status for a second time. Without Ball, the unthinkable may well have happened. Ball left Arsenal in December 1976 and enjoyed a successful spell at Southampton. He ended his playing days in America, before going into management, including two stints a Portsmouth. Awarded an MBE in 2000 for his services to football, Ball died in 2007, aged 61.

ABOVE With actress Pauline Peart during a squad visit to Pinewood Studios, February 1972.

> " *I remember thinking that he must have been some player to wear those white boots – and Alan Ball was some player.*
> David O'Leary

Frank McLintock and Jimmy Greenhoff of Stoke during an FA Cup semi-final at Villa Park, April 1972.

—LEGENDS—

Bob Wilson

Mild-mannered and articulate off the pitch, Bob Wilson's on-field bravery was more in keeping with the traditional perception of goalkeepers. A dedicated student of his art, Wilson honed a technique of diving at his opponents' feet that caused him a number of injuries throughout his career. He started late as a professional player, having given up a career as a teacher, and made his Arsenal debut as an amateur in 1963 aged 22 – the last appearance made by a non-professional in the top flight. Moreover, the £6,000 that Arsenal paid for him was the first time an amateur had commanded a transfer fee.

Wilson was forced to bide his time as understudy to Jim Furnell, but he was rewarded for his patience in 1968 when he was drafted into the first team. In 1970 he won the Fairs Cup and the following year was an ever-present in Arsenal's Double-winning side, also landing the club's Player of the Year award. He became eligible to play for Scotland when the rules were changed to allow players to play for their parents' country of origin, and he appeared twice for the Tartan Army.

The end of Wilson's playing career in 1974 did not signal the end of his Arsenal days. Wilson was the club's goalkeeping coach for 28 years, combining this with a successful broadcasting career. More recently he created the Willow Foundation, in memory of his daughter Anna, who died in 1998. In 2007 he received an OBE.

FOOTBALL —STATS—

Bob Wilson

Name: Robert Primrose Wilson

Born: 1941

Playing Career: 1962-1974

Clubs: Arsenal

Arsenal Appearances: 308

Scotland Appearances: 2

TOP The Wilson family on the Highbury pitch, September 1969.

MIDDLE Wilson and team-mates (plus Bertie Mee to Wilson's right) play Dad's Army, 1972.

BOTTOM Wilson clutches the ball during the 1971 FA Cup final.

Arsenal were unable to build upon their Double success, and during the next few years the club lost a series of influential players including Jon Sammels, Charlie George, Frank McLintock and Ray Kennedy. Don Howe, whose tactical knowledge had dovetailed perfectly with the qualities of Bertie Mee, also left for West Bromwich Albion as Arsenal spiralled into mid-table mediocrity. In 1972 they reached the FA Cup final, but lost to Leeds, and over the next four years they reached their lowest ebb since the days of Billy Wright, culminating with a lowly 17th place finish in 1976.

Mac's misery..

Beaten and bowed . . . Arsenal skipper Frank McLintock alone in his misery after Arsenal's yielding the Cup to Leeds at Wembley.

ABOVE RIGHT Leeds players celebrate Clarke's winning goal.

RIGHT Leeds's Allan Clarke battles for the ball with Peter Simpson during the 1972 FA Cup final. Simpson was a mainstay of the Arsenal side for most of the late '60s and early '70s.

TOP Goalkeeper Jimmy Rimmer, who served between the posts at Highbury from 1974 to 1976.

LEFT A bare-chested man is arrested by police after running on to the pitch during a league match between Arsenal and Manchester City at Highbury, March 1974.

TOP Barcelona's Johan Cruyff during George Armstrong's testimonial at Highbury, March 1974.

BACKGROUND A view from the Clock End terrace, Highbury, November 1979.

OPPOSITE AND ABOVE Left to right: John Matthew, Liam Brady, Brian Hornsby, and Wilf Rostron. Four of Arsenal's promising youth team players are pictured during a training session at London Colney, March 1975.

127

TOP AND ABOVE Action from two matches at

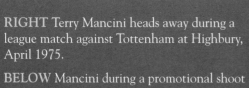

RIGHT Terry Mancini heads away during a league match against Tottenham at Highbury, April 1975.

BELOW Mancini during a promotional shoot at Wembley Stadium, February 1975. Mancini was signed by Arsenal as a replacement for Frank McLintock and went on to spend two seasons at the club. He was a true character with a taste for high jinks, including donning a wig during a game for Queens Park Rangers to disguise himself.

Tottenham's Willie Young and Malcolm McDonald during a 2-2 draw at White Hart Lane, December 1976.

Young, who would later sign for Arsenal, is sent off following the incident.

TOP, MIDDLE AND BOTTOM Arsenal goalkeeper Jimmy Rimmer is held back from confronting Willie Young by a linesman during a fractious north London derby.

CLOUGH FOR ARSENAL?

Venables snubs Arsenal

By NIGEL CLARKE

TERRY VENABLES, Crystal Palace's talented coach, has turned down an offer of around £25,000 from Arsenal to become their new manager.

The job, which carries probably the highest salary in club football, was offered to him last week.

Venables, on holiday in Majorca with his family, was approached by a Highbury representative who flew out from London to see him.

His decision to say "No" now means he is almost certain to stay at Selhurst Park and take over as manager from Malcolm Allison.

Chasing

And it still leaves Arsenal searching for a replacement for Bertie Mee who stepped down almost three months ago. Palace and Norwich are chasing Mark Nightingale, Bournemouth's talented teenage midfield player.

But Palace are favourites to sign him. For their offer of a player —Peter Johnson—plus a cash adjustment of £8,000 is more suitable to Bournemouth

BYE, BYE BERTIE...

ARSENAL LINE UP SMITH

ARSENAL'S directors sit down in ten days' time to discuss the appointment of a new manager.

This follows yesterday's decision by Bertie Mee to retire at the end of the season.

Mee, who ranked alongside the legendary Herbert Chapman as the club's most successful manager, quit because of the pressures in a job he had held for ten years.

Yet Arsenal know that only a few of the country's managers would reject the chance to take over at Highbury—almost the No. 10 Downing Street of football.

The club were quick to stress last night that no early replacement was likely and no moves had yet been made to find a new man.

But those figuring in last night's inevitable speculation were two ex-Arsenal players: Jimmy Bloomfield, Leicester's progressive and popular manager, Stoke's George Eastham, who has managed the England Under-23 side, and Alan Dicks, who seems likely to steer Bristol City to promotion.

"It was no surprise to me when Bertie advised us of his decision on Monday," said chairman Denis Hill Wood.

"It was because of the pressures of the job and that at Arsenal the manager is never right, always wrong.

"Results obviously

Bertie Mee . . . the pressures of managing Arsenal were intense.

Bloomfield could head queue to succeed him

had a bearing on his decision and I emphasise it was his decision."

Mee, 57, took over from Billy Wright in 1966 —after joining the club as physiotherapist six years earlier.

He then rebuilt Arsenal's fading glory with the help of the brilliant coaching of Don Howe and in 1971 Arsenal became only the second club in this century to achieve the

League and FA Cup double.

After Howe's departure Arsenal's fortunes never again rose to such heights.

Mee's selling of Frank McLintock, Charlie George, Ray Kennedy and Jeff Blockley has been a constant source of controversy — all four having made a success at their new clubs.

On his own admission Mee is a man who shows

little emotion — being the only manager I know of refusing to talk about matches until 24 hours afterwards.

For that reason he gained respect rather than affection, but no one can dispute his record.

Last Saturday's 6—1 victory over West Ham at Highbury speeded up Mee's decision — he felt Arsenal had turned the corner

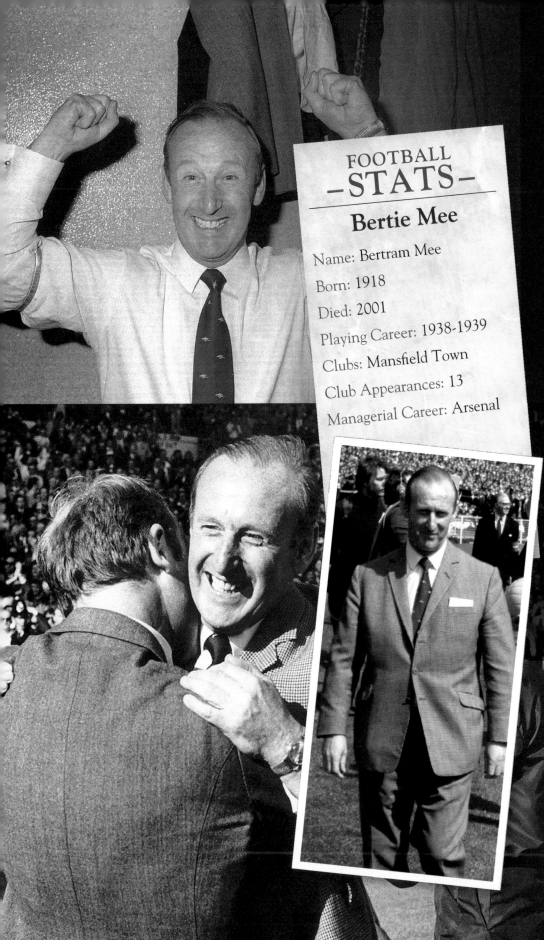

–LEGENDS–

Bertie Mee

FOOTBALL –STATS–

Bertie Mee

Name: Bertram Mee

Born: 1918

Died: 2001

Playing Career: 1938-1939

Clubs: Mansfield Town

Club Appearances: 13

Managerial Career: Arsenal

A former servant in the Royal Army Medical Corps and boasting an inglorious playing career with Mansfield Town, Bertie Mee is one of the more unlikely success stories in the annals of British football management. In 1970 he led Arsenal to their first major trophy in 17 years – the Fairs Cup – and a year later he became only the second boss of the 20th century to win the coveted League and FA Cup Double. These achievements were all the more remarkable given he was promoted from the role of club physiotherapist.

Having achieved the Double, Mee seemed to have laid the foundations for a period of domination, but somehow this never happened. After finishing as runners-up to Liverpool in 1973 they declined alarmingly in the league. Mee, hurt by the growing criticism, resigned in 1976. Later he served as general manager at Watford and was credited for discovering John Barnes. He was made an OBE in 1984 for services to football and died in 2001, aged 82.

TOP Mee celebrating Arsenal's league title victory in the dressing room at White Hart Lane, May 1971.

LEFT Embracing coach Don Howe after completing the Double at Wembley.

133

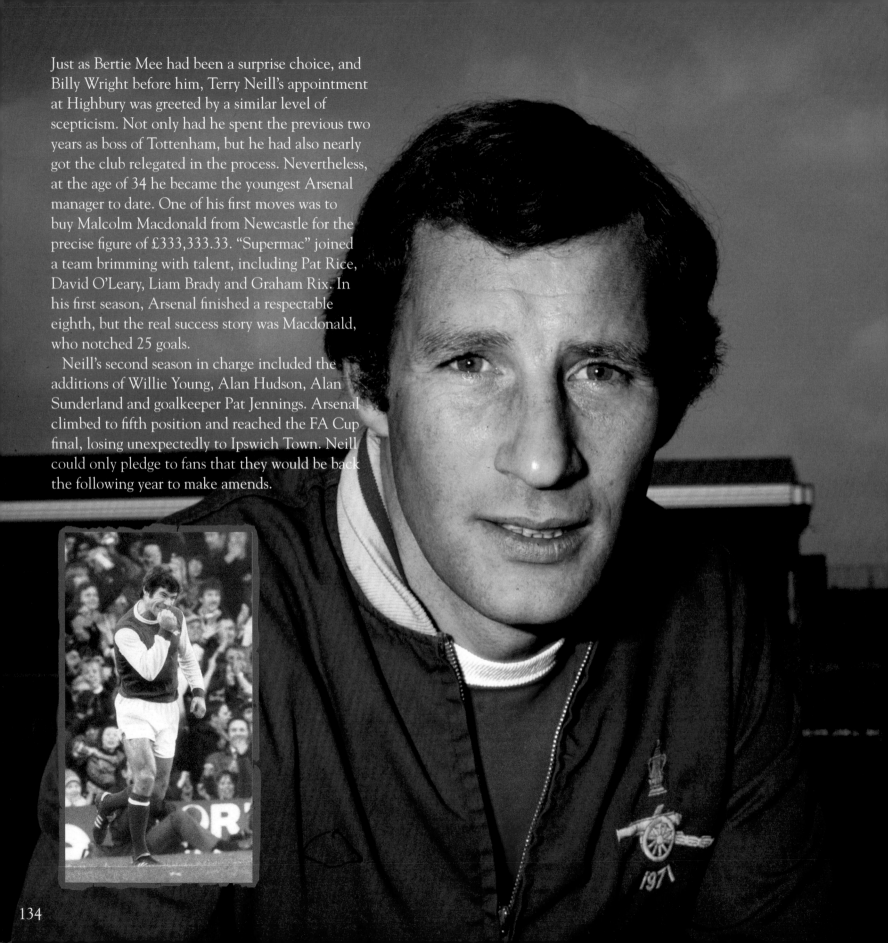

Just as Bertie Mee had been a surprise choice, and Billy Wright before him, Terry Neill's appointment at Highbury was greeted by a similar level of scepticism. Not only had he spent the previous two years as boss of Tottenham, but he had also nearly got the club relegated in the process. Nevertheless, at the age of 34 he became the youngest Arsenal manager to date. One of his first moves was to buy Malcolm Macdonald from Newcastle for the precise figure of £333,333.33. "Supermac" joined a team brimming with talent, including Pat Rice, David O'Leary, Liam Brady and Graham Rix. In his first season, Arsenal finished a respectable eighth, but the real success story was Macdonald, who notched 25 goals.

Neill's second season in charge included the additions of Willie Young, Alan Hudson, Alan Sunderland and goalkeeper Pat Jennings. Arsenal climbed to fifth position and reached the FA Cup final, losing unexpectedly to Ipswich Town. Neill could only pledge to fans that they would be back the following year to make amends.

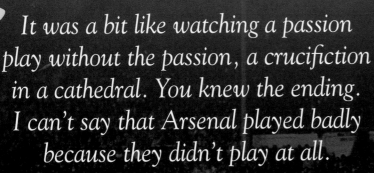

> "It was a bit like watching a passion play without the passion, a crucifiction in a cathedral. You knew the ending. I can't say that Arsenal played badly because they didn't play at all.
>
> *Arsenal fan, quoted in the Daily Mirror after the 1978 defeat to Ipswich*

GLOOM AND

DESPAIR: Young Arsenal supporter David Lennon sits in a deserted Wembley after travelling all the way from Dublin.

OPPOSITE Terry Neill, August 1976.

OPPOSITE BELOW Malcolm Macdonald celebrates after scoring for Arsenal against former club Newcastle at Highbury.

ABOVE Action from Arsenal's 1978 FA Cup final defeat to Ipswich.

RIGHT Ipswich players celebrate at the final whistle.

–LEGENDS–

George Armstrong

Armstrong's arrival at Highbury, straight from school in his native County Durham, came at a time when the traditional winger seemed close to extinction. But the man commonly known as "Geordie" kept the specialist role alive, tearing full-backs apart down both flanks and creating endless chances for grateful team-mates. Such was his effectiveness, it was estimated that he contributed more than half the goals scored in the Double-winning season of 1970/71.

Unfortunately for Armstrong, the England coach at the time, Alf Ramsey, was one of those who considered the wide-man an anachronism, and so international recognition eluded him. Having spent 15 full seasons at Arsenal, Armstrong left the club for Leicester City in 1977 before going into coaching at Aston Villa, Fulham and then the Kuwaiti National Team. He returned to Highbury in 1990 as part of the Reserve team staff, but he died suddenly on the Arsenal training ground in 2000, aged 56.

FOOTBALL –STATS–

George Armstrong

Name: George Armstrong

Born: 1944

Died: 2000

Playing Career: 1961-1979

Clubs: Arsenal, Leicester City, Stockport County

Arsenal Appearances: 621

Goals: 68

Managerial Career: Enderby Town, FK Mjølner, Kuwait

ABOVE In the kitchen displaying his eggs-between-fingers party trick, January 1975.

The 1979 FA Cup Final

On an uncomfortably hot day at Wembley in May 1979, one of the FA Cup's greatest ever finals saw Arsenal secure their only major trophy of Terry Neill's seven-year reign. Manchester United were their opponents and in the first half the Northerners were overwhelmed by Liam Brady's guile and Brian Talbot's midfield running. Two goals from Talbot and Frank Stapleton put Arsenal in a dominant position, but drama was in store.

With just five minutes remaining the game was transformed as two scrappy goals brought United level. But there was more to come. From kick-off, Brady took the ball deep into United's half and released Rix on the left. The winger crossed to the far post and Alan Sunderland slid the ball home for the winner.

TOP to bottom (left to right): Pat Jennings, Pat Rice, Sammy Nelson, David Price, Willie Young, David O'Leary, Brian Talbot, Graham Rix, Frank Stapleton, Steve Walford, Liam Brady and Alan Sunderland.

ABOVE Alan Sunderland (number 8) celebrates after scoring the dramatic 89th minute winner in thee 1979 FA Cup final

LEFT Frank Stapleton shields the ball during the final.

OPPOSITE Prince Charles presents the FA Cup to captain Pat Rice.

RIGHT Alan Sunderland with his winner's medal.

139

Anarchy in the UK

ABOVE Suspected football hooligans being searched after clashes between Arsenal and Manchester United fans, August 1979.

OPPOSITE Sammy Nelson gives Arsenal fans an eyeful during a match against Coventry at Highbury, April 1979. Nelson's gesture came after he had scored an equalizing goal, having been barracked by the crowd for putting the ball into his own net in the first half. He was fined and suspended for two weeks by the club.

FOOTBALL
–STATS–

Pat Rice

Name: Patrick James Rice

Born: 1949

Playing Career: 1964-1984

Clubs: Arsenal, Watford

Arsenal Appearances: 528

Goals: 12

Northern Ireland
Appearances: 49

Goals: 1

–LEGENDS–

Pat Rice

Though born in Belfast, Rice grew up in London, and after working at a greengrocers on Gillespie Road near Highbury, he joined the Gunners as an apprentice in 1964. He turned professional in 1966, making his first-team debut in December 1967. Playing at right-back, Rice was initially a bit-part player, making only 16 appearances in his first three seasons. In September 1968, before he was even a regular at Arsenal, he won his first cap for Northern Ireland.

Rice got his chance to establish himself at the start of the 1970/71 season, when first choice right-back Peter Storey was moved into central midfield, and he played in almost every game of that Double-winning campaign. He finally left Arsenal in 1980 to join Watford, aged 31. After ending his playing career, he moved into coaching and returned to Highbury in 1984 as youth team coach. After winning the FA Youth Cup twice, he was promoted to assistant first-team coach and also served briefly as caretaker manager, winning all three league matches in charge. He remains at the club to this day.

OPPOSITE LEFT Lifting the FA Cup in 1979.

OPPOSITE RIGHT Rice does a turn as a traffic warden.

ABOVE Conducting the orchestra at Highbury.

143

> " You'll see a differe[nt]
> Arsenal in Brussel[s].
> That's a promise.
> Pat Rice

[1]980 Cup Defeats

[Yo]ungster Paul Allen is cynically
[brought down?] as he bares down on goal during
[the final a]t Wembley.

[The Profe]ssional Foul rule not yet in
[force, so just?] a caution. Second Division
[West Ham won] the match 1-0.

> "I hope Graham Rix doesn't carry any burden with him for the miss. He has been one of the major forces of getting us here, and he was outstanding tonight."
>
> Terry Neill

Mirror Sport

Thursday, May 15, 1980   No. 23,718
Telephone: (STD code 01)—353 0246

KICK OF DEATH!

TOP The two goalkeepers, Pat Jennings of Arsenal and Pereira of Valencia, before the penalty shoot-out to decide the 1980 European Cup Winners' Cup final at Heysel Stadium, Brussels. Liam Brady, with his normally magical left foot, and Valencia's Argentinian legend Mario Kempes both missed their kicks, before Graham Rix's shot was saved to give the Spanish club victory and Arsenal their second Cup final defeat in four days.

RIGHT A dejected Rix walks away after his penalty miss as the Valencia team celebrate.

The Signing That Never Was

Clive Allen, the 19-year-old teenager, signs for Arsenal from Queens Park Rangers for £1,250,000 in the summer of 1980. But just two months later, having not played a single competitive match, he was sold in part-exchange to Crystal Palace with full-back Kenny Sansom coming the other way. No official explanation has ever been given, but an oft-stated theory is that QPR and Crystal Palace had secured a deal for Allen on the condition that QPR did not sell Allen to Palace directly, and Arsenal acted as go-betweens. Another suggests that Terry Neill changed his opinion of the player after watching him in pre-season friendlies.

Clive Allen and England full-back Kenny Sansom.

Pelé At Highbury

RIGHT Brazil legend Pelé on the Highbury pitch during half-time in a match between Arsenal and Aston Villa, May 1980. A 2-0 victory for Arsenal did not stop Aston Villa securing the League Championship the same day.

BELOW Paul Davis on the ball during the same game.

BOTTOM Aston Villa fans are held back by police after invading the pitch to celebrate their title triumph.

ABOVE The Metropolitan Police marching band perform their traditional half-time routine during a game against West Bromwich Albion, April 1980.

OPPOSITE Even the half-time entertainment couldn't lift the gloom of a depressing era for Arsenal fans. In a sign of the times, the Ipswich goalkeeper looks distinctly untroubled during a game at Highbury, December 1980.

–LEGENDS–

Liam Brady

Brady was the complete attacking midfielder, blessed with skill, vision, balance, strength, a fine shot and a graceful turn of speed that allowed him to glide past opponents. He turned professional on his 17th birthday in 1973 and when Alan Ball left Highbury in 1976, Brady took up the midfield reins. The Irishman helped drag Arsenal from their mid-Seventies slump to reach three successive FA Cup finals between 1978 and 1980. That first year, Brady scored one of his most memorable goals against Tottenham at White Hart Lane in a 5-0 victory – a curling left foot shot from the edge of the penalty area.

A year later he was Man of the Match at Wembley as Arsenal beat Manchester United in the FA Cup final, and also won the PFA Player of the Year award. But a bombshell was coming: Brady announced he would leave Highbury for Italian club Juventus at the end of the 1979/80 campaign. He rose to the new challenge, winning two Series 'A' titles while Arsenal struggled without their talisman. He returned to London to play for West Ham before retiring from playing in 1990. Later he managed Celtic and Brighton before joining the youth development academy at Arsenal which he now heads.

RIGHT Brady at a charity boxing match, September 1979.

BACKGROUND Putting his magical left foot into practice, March 1980.

FOOTBALL –STATS–

Liam Brady

Name: Liam Brady

Born: 1956

Playing Career: 1973-1990

Clubs: Arsenal, Juventus, Sampdoria, Inter Milan, Ascoli, West Ham United

Arsenal Appearances: 307

Goals: 59

Republic of Ireland Appearances: 72

Goals: 9

Managerial Career: Celtic, Brighton & Hove Albion

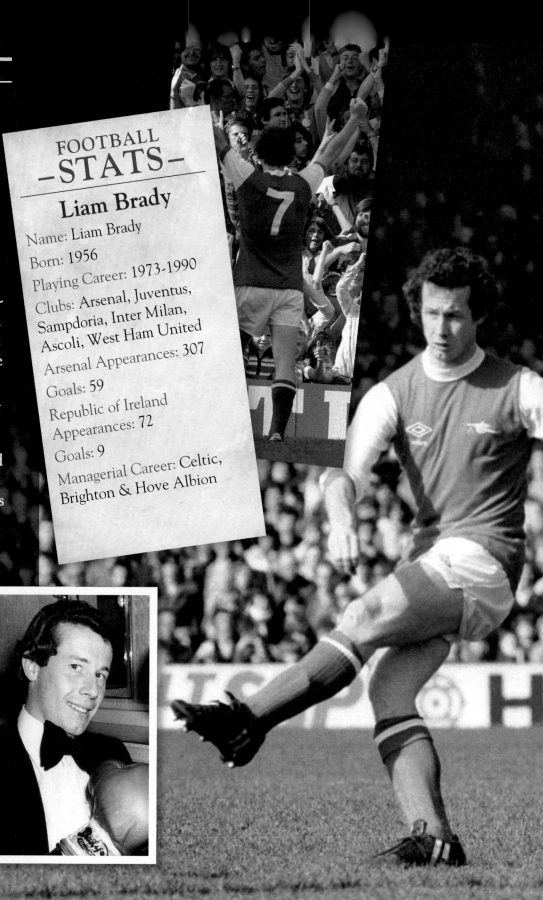

FAR LEFT Peter Hill-Wood, who took over as Arsenal chairman in 1982 after the death of his father, Denis, who had himself succeeded his own father Samuel. As the long family custodianship of the club continued, one of the new chairman's first decisions was to sack manager Terry Neill, who had presided over a series of embarrassing cup defeats to Middlesbrough, York, Oxford and Walsall.

LEFT Don Howe, initially named caretaker manager after Neill was sacked, took up the appointment permanently in April 1984.

BELOW Charlie Nicholas, signed by Terry Neill six months before he was sacked, during an away game at Stoke City, January 1984. This was the first season in which Arsenal had a sponsor – JVC – on their shirt.

Graham Rix during an FA Cup match against Bolton Wanderers at Highbury, January 1983. After the departure of Brady to Juventus, many believed the gifted Rix would also leave, but he stayed at the club, and became captain in 1983.

FOOTBALL STATS–

Pat Jennings

Name: Patrick Anthony Jennings

Born: 1945

Playing Career: 1963-1985

Clubs: Watford, Tottenham Hotspur, Arsenal

Arsenal Appearances: 327

Goals: 1

Northern Ireland Appearances: 119

Pat Jennings

Calm and assured, Pat Jennings's positional sense meant he rarely needed to resort to the spectacular. Instead he would effortlessly pluck crosses out of the air or push shots aside with his famously giant hands. He accomplished many great things in his career, including a record 119 caps for Northern Ireland and more than 1,000 club appearances, but arguably his finest achievement was gaining the unanimous and enduring affection of both Arsenal and Tottenham fans.

In 1977 Spurs manager Keith Burkinshaw decided Jennings was past his best and let him leave for Arsenal for a cut-price fee. His first three seasons at Highbury ended with appearances in the FA Cup final, although only the 1979 showpiece yielded a winner's medal. Jennings found himself out of favour in 1982, but he bounced back and regained his starting place until his retirement. His long career ended in style at the age of 41 as he represented Northern Ireland at the 1986 World Cup finals in Mexico. It was a fitting finale for one of football's greatest ever goalkeepers.

RIGHT Holding a football to mark his 1,000th club appearance, February 1983.

BACKGROUND Diving at the feet of a Tottenham player.

RIGHT John Lukic during a league game against Sheffield Wednesday, September 1985.

BELOW Jennings and his understudy, November 1984. Lukic would replace him as first choice goalkeeper the same season.

RIGHT A pitch invader is chased by a helmet-wielding policeman during a match with Tottenham at Highbury, January 1985.

BELOW Paul Davis helps form a wall during a league match with Aston Villa, October 1985.

The End Game
1986-1992

Arsenal manager George Graham.

1986 George Graham is appointed manager following the resignation of Don Howe. **1986** The club celebrates its centenary. **1987** Graham wins the League Cup in his first season against Liverpool. **1988** Arsenal lose the League Cup final to Luton Town. **1989** On a day that Arsenal beat Newcastle 1-0 at Highbury, the Hillsborough Disaster occurs in which 96 Liverpool fans die. **1989** Arsenal win the league title on goal difference, beating Liverpool at Anfield by two goals to nil in the final game of the season. **1991** Arsenal win the league title, losing one game all season. **1991** Arsenal announce a bond scheme to finance the club's stadium redevelopment in adherence to the Taylor Report. **1992** The North Bank terrace is demolished to make way for a 12,500 capacity all-seater stand.

Niall Quinn and Charlie Nicholas wheel away
in celebration after Quinn's winning goal against
Southampton at Highbury, December 1986.

ABOVE George Graham returns to Arsenal as manager after three years in charge at Millwall, March 1986. He replaced Don Howe, who asked to be released from his contract amid rumours that Arsenal were interested in Barcelona boss Terry Venables.

TOP LEFT Perry Groves tussles for the ball in a match against West Ham, November 1986. Groves was George Graham's first signing and became a cult hero at Highbury.

OPPOSITE TOP Players of Arsenal's past attend the club's centenary celebrations at Highbury, December 1986.

OPPOSITE BOTTOM Charlie Nicholas is given the magic sponge treatment during a match against Luton Town at Highbury, February 1986.

George Graham was quick to clear out much of the old guard and lay down new standards of discipline throughout the club, much like Bertie Mee had done. The effects were immediate: in September 1986 they embarked on a 22-game unbeaten run, putting them top of the league at Christmas, though they would eventually tail off to finish fourth.

Clearing snow off the terraces at Highbury, January 1987.

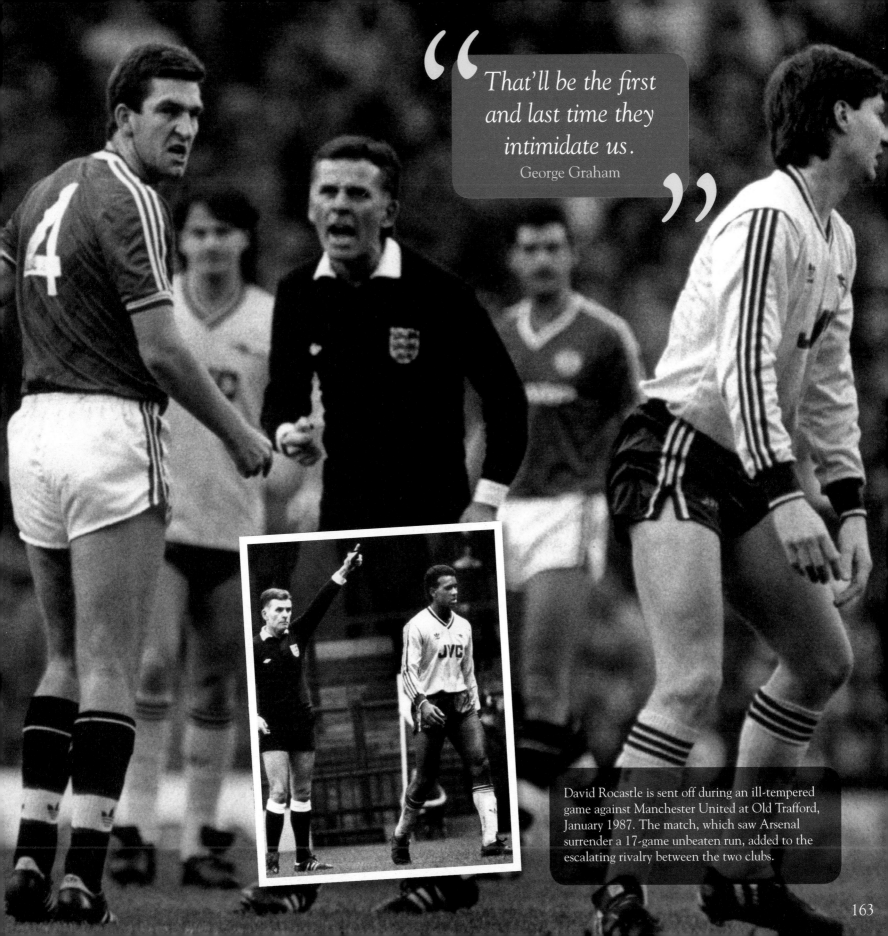

> "That'll be the first and last time they intimidate us."
> George Graham

David Rocastle is sent off during an ill-tempered game against Manchester United at Old Trafford, January 1987. The match, which saw Arsenal surrender a 17-game unbeaten run, added to the escalating rivalry between the two clubs.

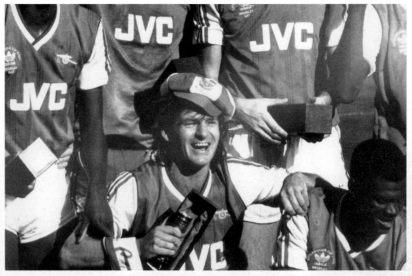

The 1987 League Cup Final

Even in light of an epic 2-1 victory over Tottenham in the semi-finals that demonstrated the club's new-found resilience under George Graham, Arsenal went into the final against Liverpool as underdogs. And when Ian Rush scored the opening goal, history was against them too: a remarkable 150 games had passed without Liverpool losing a game when Rush scored.

But the omens did not reckon for Arsenal's new spirit. Charlie Nicholas equalized on the stroke of half-time and with seven minutes remaining Perry Groves left defenders in his wake down the left, squared the ball to Nicholas, whose weak shot took a spinning deflection and trickled into the net. Graham had his first trophy – the first of many.

> "Here I was, a ginger-haired nobody, setting up the winning goal for Arsenal."
>
> Perry Groves

TOP LEFT Tony Adams and Charlie Nicholas celebrate Nicholas's equalizer against Liverpool at Wembley, April 1987.

TOP RIGHT Two-goal hero Nicholas revels in victory.

ABOVE Graham with the trophy back at Highbury.

MIRROR SPORT

Charlie bubbles

SELL ME IF YOU DARE

GUNNERS GRAB GLORY

■ SUCCESS goes to Charlie Nicholas's head after his two-goal Littlewoods Cup Triumph at Wembley.

Picture: MONTE FRESCO

CHARLIE NICHOLAS yesterday grabbed the Wembley glory goals that spelled out to Arsenal: "Sell me if you dare!"

Then he admitted: "I want to stay at Highbury."

Charlie used the Littlewoods Cup Final as a platform to prove he has a future at the club.

And after the 2-1 victory over Liverpool, he said: "I think Arsenal have already made up their minds what they want.

"I've got to sort things out with manager George Graham.

"There are no problems on the financial side—it's the football aspect that we have to talk about."

Nicholas's contract is up this summer, and they have just paid £750,000 for striker Alan Smith from Leicester.

But if Arsenal now decide to let Champagne Charlie move on, there will be an outcry from his adoring fans.

He added: "This was my most satisfying performance at the club. And it's taken me four years to get a trophy.

"There have been bad

By NIGEL CLARKE

times, but this is the best day I've had since I came to London."

Nicholas scored in the 30th minute — "just a tap-in from four yards, my distance" — then got the winner with a deflection off Ronnie Whelan eight minutes from time.

He explained: "I shot for one corner and the ball went in the other. It was a bit fortunate, but they all count."

Graham said: "Charlie was magnificent. But I don't want to talk about a new contract. It's a personal thing."

And he added: "It's time to bury the 'lucky Arsenal' tag. There's nothing lucky about what we have achieved."

CHARLIE'S CROWN JEWELS — See pages 26, 27

Published by Mirror Group Newspapers (1986) Ltd. (01-353 0246) and printed by British Newspaper Printing Corporation (London) Ltd., Holborn Circus, London EC1P 1DQ. Registered at the Post Office as a news

LEGENDS

Charlie Nicholas

The soon-to-be-crowned Darling of the North Bank arrived at Highbury in June 1983 as a beacon of hope amid a sea of mediocrity. Arsenal had struggled to challenge for trophies since the departure of Liam Brady three years earlier, and were in desperate need of a spark to reignite the club's ambitions. The Scottish forward came with a formidable reputation, having hit an incredible 50 goals for Celtic the previous season and fresh from rejecting the advances of heavyweights Liverpool and Manchester United. With his artistry and personality, Nicholas connected with fans and his hedonistic reputation only enhanced his cult appeal.

However, Nicholas could not bring the trophies that his new fans craved. His extravagant skills were let down by a lack of consistency, and when George Graham arrived as manager in 1986 it marked the beginning of the end. As players, Nicholas and Graham were cut from the same casual cloth, but Graham the manager was a different proposition and the laid-back Nicholas was at odds with the ethos Graham wanted to foster.

Before his departure Nicholas had a final trick up his sleeve – a Wembley brace to beat Liverpool in the League Cup final, winning Arsenal their first trophy in eight years. He was sold to Aberdeen in 1988, retired in 1996 and **is** now a television pundit.

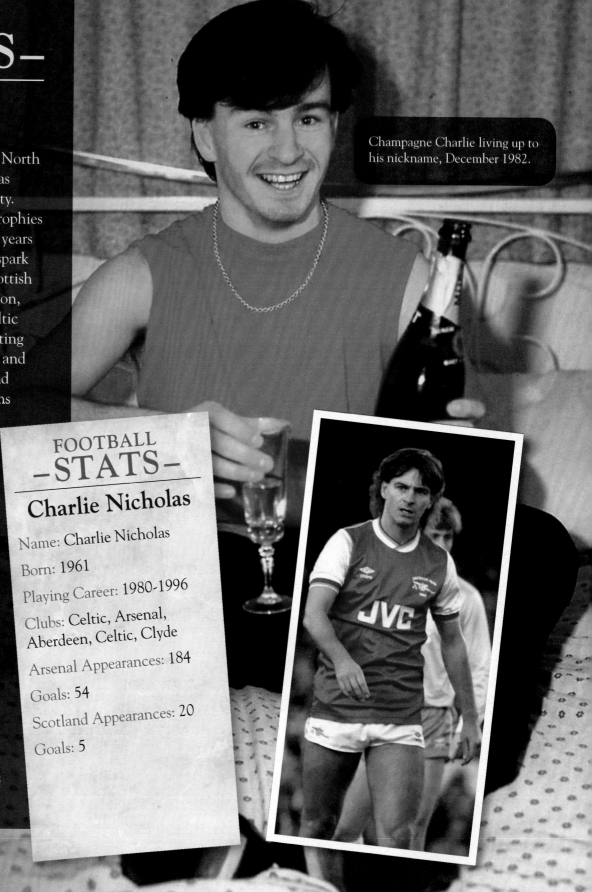

Champagne Charlie living up to his nickname, December 1982.

FOOTBALL –STATS–

Charlie Nicholas

Name: Charlie Nicholas

Born: 1961

Playing Career: 1980-1996

Clubs: Celtic, Arsenal, Aberdeen, Celtic, Clyde

Arsenal Appearances: 184

Goals: 54

Scotland Appearances: 20

Goals: 5

The 1988 League Cup Final

ABOVE Danny Wilson equalizes for Luton in the League Cup final at Wembley, April 1988.

BELOW Brian Stein celebrates his winning goal in the final minute to give Luton the first trophy in their history.

Defender Gus Caesar ahead of the 1988 final. Like Ian Ure before him, Wembley Stadium would prove an unhappy stomping ground for Caesar, who miskicked a clearance in his own penalty area, allowing Wilson to bundle the ball into the net. He played just five more matches for Arsenal in two seasons, eventually leaving the club in 1991 on a free transfer.

167

–LEGENDS–

Kenny Sansom

Sansom was already an established England international when he arrived at Highbury from Crystal Palace in 1980, as part of a swap-deal with Clive Allen. He quickly gained the left-back spot from Sammy Nelson and continued to develop as a player despite Arsenal's struggles during that decade. Sansom was a precise passer and had remarkable pace over short distances. He was strong in the air, despite his small stature, and his reluctance to go to ground – preferring instead to dispossess opponents through guile – meant his white shorts were often left unblemished.

Sansom was named captain in 1987 and led the team out at Wembley that year as they beat Liverpool to win the League Cup. It was the only club trophy he would win during his career, though he also earned vast international acclaim – his 86 England caps remaining a record for a full-back.

In 1988, Sansom's relationship with manager George Graham soured and he was replaced as captain by a young Tony Adams. He was sold in December of that year to Newcastle – one of six clubs he played for until his retirement in 1995.

ABOVE During an England training session.
OPPOSITE Nailing his political colours to the mast.

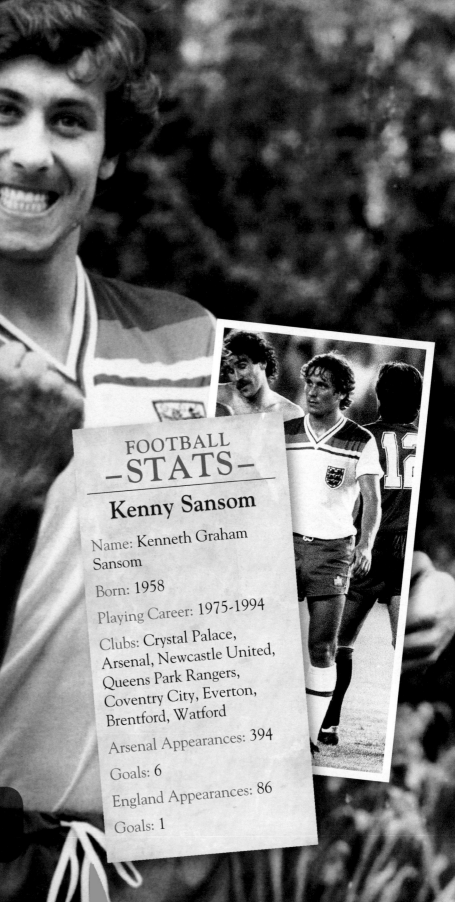

FOOTBALL –STATS–

Kenny Sansom

Name: Kenneth Graham Sansom

Born: 1958

Playing Career: 1975-1994

Clubs: Crystal Palace, Arsenal, Newcastle United, Queens Park Rangers, Coventry City, Everton, Brentford, Watford

Arsenal Appearances: 394

Goals: 6

England Appearances: 86

Goals: 1

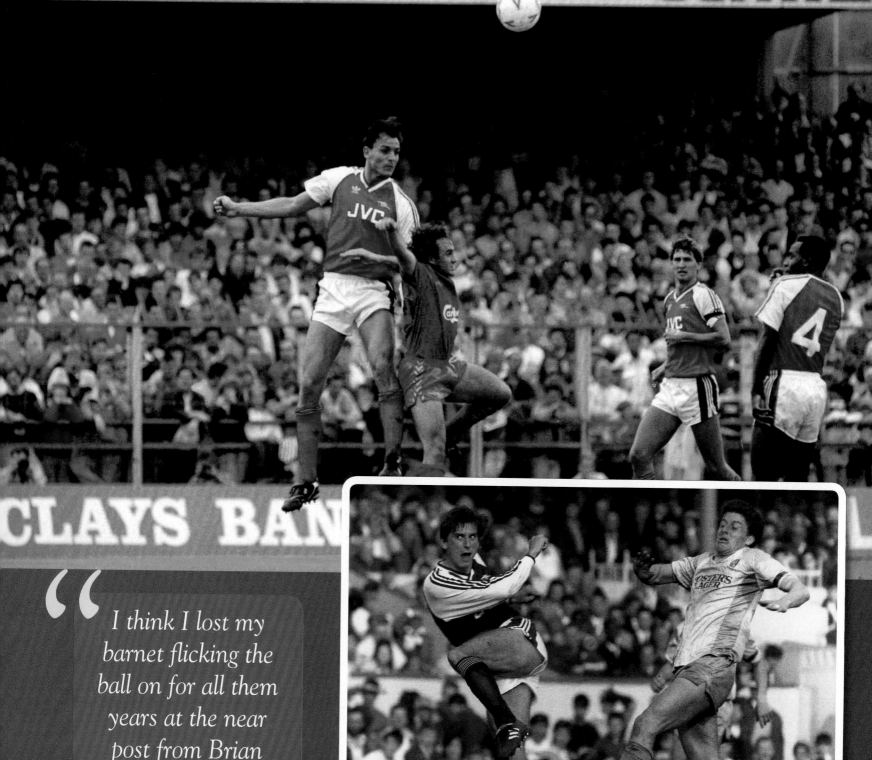

> *I think I lost my barnet flicking the ball on for all them years at the near post from Brian Marwood's corners.*
>
> Steve Bould

LEFT Steve Bould heads clear during the opening game of the 1988/89 season against Wimbledon that Arsenal won 5-1.

BELOW LEFT Alan Smith scores against Norwich at Highbury as Arsenal close in on the title with a 5-0 victory, May 1989.

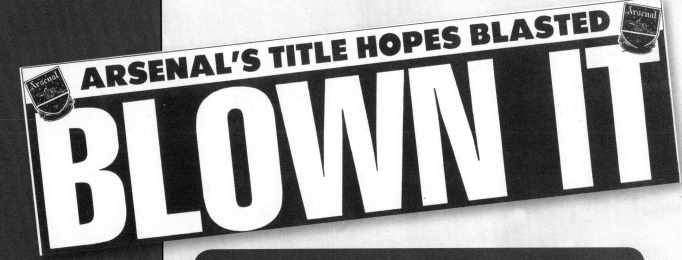

ARSENAL'S TITLE HOPES BLASTED
BLOWN IT

ABOVE The *Daily Mirror* headline after a 2-2 draw with Wimbledon at Highbury that left Arsenal's title hopes looking all but over, May 1989.

BELOW The league table and remaining fixtures as the 1989 title run-in reaches a dramatic climax. Liverpool's 5-1 thrashing of West Ham left Arsenal needing to win by two clear goals at Anfield in a game delayed until Friday 26th May after the Hillsborough Disaster.

LEE DIXON and David Rocastle celebrate after Rocastle had scored Arsenal's fifth goal. Picture: ARNOLD SLATER

TITLE FIGHT

	P	W	D	L	F	A	Pts
Arsenal	37	21	10	6	71	36	73
Liverpool	36	21	10	5	60	25	73
Nottm For.	37	17	13	7	63	41	64

Remaining matches:
May 23: Liverpool v West Ham
May 26: Liverpool v Arsenal

The 1989 League Title Decider

Bolstered by lower-division purchases and bargain buys including Steve Bould, Lee Dixon and Nigel Winterburn, George Graham's young side led the league until the final few games of the season. Then the wheels fell off. A consecutive home defeat and a draw left Arsenal with the seemingly impossible task of beating Liverpool by two clear goals on the Merseysiders' own turf to claim the title. Their prospects seemed even more remote given Liverpool's incentive of playing for the memories of those who died at Hillsborough, not to mention the League and FA Cup Double.

On the day of the game, it was reported that the launch of BSkyB, the Rupert Murdoch satellite channel, had been delayed by technical problems. It would be this match at Anfield that would convince TV executives of the vast, untapped potential of live football on television as record numbers flocked to watch the title decider on a Friday night. No one knew it at the time, but just a few years later the way football was sold, marketed and watched would be transformed forever.

TOP Alan Smith glances a second-half header to put Arsenal 1-0 up. The Liverpool players respond by surrounding the referee, claiming an infringement. After a gut-wrenching consultation with his linesman that lasted seconds but for Arsenal fans felt like hours, the goal is given.

LEFT Kevin Richardson carries a bunch of flowers to the Anfield crowd in tribute to the 96 fans who lost their lives at Hillsborough.

RIGHT Liverpool goalkeeper Bruce Grobbelaar saves at the feet of Paul Merson.

OPPOSITE BOTTOM Tony Adams clears as Ian Rush closes in.

Michael Thomas scores Arsenal's second goal in injury time to give Arsenal the title.

Thomas celebrates as Steve Nichol puts his hands to his head in disbelief.

Tony Adams offers his commiserations to John Barnes after the game.

Michael Thomas and David Rocastle parade the pitch with the Barclays trophy.

Full-back Lee Dixon enjoys the moment.

Adams lifts the trophy with John Lukic and Lee Dixon alongside him.

> "We have laid a foundation of belief at Highbury.
> George Graham

George Graham takes the acclaim of the Arsenal fans.

RIGHT A grinning George Graham passes under the famous "This is Anfield" sign, clutching his booty.

BOTTOM RIGHT An emotional David O'Leary is embraced by the boss.

It's Arsenal's crown as king Thomas

THE GREATEST

SKIP TO IT!
ARSENAL skipper Tony Adams keeps out Liverpool's ace striker Ian Rush in the championship thriller at Anfield last night

Graham night of triumph

Liverpool 0, Arsenal 2

ARSENAL last night pulled off a soccer miracle to deny Kenny Dalglish a place in history.

Dalglish was bidding to become the first manager to win the double twice, following his triumph three years ago.

Instead, in one of the most dramatic climaxes to any championship season, the Gunners proved they are worthy champions.

The North London glory boys stole the title from the clutches of the FA Cup winners with almost the last kick of this sensational and traumatic season.

Michael Thomas, who had earlier missed a golden chance, made no mistake with an injury-time goal that put the two giants level on points and goal difference, with the Gunners taking the title by scoring more goals.

Thrown

George Graham's team seemed to have thrown the championship away at least twice in recent months, but their 73 goals outstripped Liverpool's 65.

It is 90 years since two teams last went into the final match each with a realistic chance of taking the title. And this time the exhilarating climax was shared by millions of TV viewers.

ITV are paying £50 million for an exclusive contract and they got their money's worth as Arsenal clinched their first title for 18 years — the last time their current manager Graham was in their line-up.

At 10.19 last night, Graham walked off the Anfield pitch with the championship trophy firmly in his grasp, writing his name in the Highbury Hall of Fame just as he always wanted to do.

Graham had joined in Arsenal's lap of honour as some of the Arsenal players broke down with tears of joy, while some Liverpool players wept in despair.

Many Liverpool supporters stayed on the Kop to sportingly ap-

SPORTS SUMMARY

BARCLAYS LEAGUE
FIRST DIVISION
Liverpool.....(0) 0 Arsenal.......(0) 2
41,718

INTERNATIONAL
N Ireland.....(0) 0 Chile...........(1) 1
2,500   Astengo
(Windsor Park, Belfast)

GREYHOUNDS
ROMFORD.— 7.30 Lesley Honey 3-1jf (2-1, £23.07). 7.45 Triumph 11-4f (3-6, £11.85). 8.00 Monroe Sailor 2-1f (4-5, £14.96). 8.16 Edwards Surprise 3-1 (2-3, £18.67). 8.32 Barrowboys Town 4-1 (3-6, £20.44). 8.48 Precious Chimes 100-30 (6-2, £20.56). 9.04 Silkys Parade 4-1 (6-4, £35.31). 9.21 Poor Form 4-1 (2-9, £28.03). 9.39 Borris Nap 5-2f (1-5, £14.53). 9.56 Ballymeath Lad 10-11f (1-3, £8.44). 10.13 River Loch 5-4 (1-2, £6.25). Nrs: King Paddy (3), Orlas Wendy 12-1

PONTEFRACT:
Good to firm
6.45:CHAMPAGNE GOLD (T Ives, 5-2f) 1; Croft Imperial (4-1) 2; Tadeus (9-2) 3. 5 ran. 2½, 2 (Denys Smith) Tote: £3.10; £1.50, £1.90; Df: £3.50; Csf: £11.25.
7.10: MY DIAMOND RING (R Fox, 6-1f) 1; Chic-Anita (20-1) 2; My Concordia (20-1) 3; Weffie (9-1) 4. 21 ran. 1½, 1½ (M Usher) Tote: £5.30; £1.80, £2.90, £3.30, £2.30; Df: £49.60; Csf: £112.93; Tricast: £2,057.06. Nr: Cretan Boy.
7.35: ROSEATE LODGE (W Carson, 11-10f) 1; Mystery Band (10-1) 2; Chorai Sundown (9-2) 3; Bachelor's Pet (50-1) 4. 16 ran. 4, sh hd (J Watts) Tote: £2.40; £1.10, £1.90, £1.60, £10.50; Df: £11.60; Csf: £15.64; Tricast: £45.60.
8.05: REGAL REFORM (Dean McKeown, 9-1) 1; Austhorpe Sunset (4-1)jf 2; Sunset Reins Free (11-1) 3; Quip (33-1) 4. Amazing Silks 4jf 17 ran. 6, ½ (G Moore) Tote: £28.20;

Ace Pat sacked

By IAN GIBB

PAT VAN DEN HAUWE was sacked by Wales last night — and manager Terry Yorath stormed: "He'll never play for me again."

Van Den Hauwe, one of Everton's best players in last Saturday's FA Cup final defeat by Liverpool, is

CHELSEA PENSION

By IAN GIBB
STAMFORD BRIDGE boss Bobby Campbell can stay at Chelsea until he draws his pension,

Palace storm

● CRYSTAL Palace have upset Blackburn by switching the home leg of their Second Division play-off final for a second time.

● Originally set for Saturday June 3, it was put back 24 hours because it clashed with England's World Cup tie against Poland at Wembley.

● But it has now reverted to the Saturday on police advice.

flattens sad Liverpool in injury time

STORY EVER TOLD!

MIRACLE MEN KOP TITLE

By HARRY HARRIS

cally turning on everyone who has accused them of negative tactics.

The Gunners have won the championship by scoring eight more goals than Liverpool, with Graham putting the emphasis on entertaining football.

Arsenal dropped home points against Sheffield Wednesday, Millwall, Nottingham Forest and Charlton, but really looked to have thrown away the title with self-inflicted wounds — squandering five points in their last two Highbury games, losing to Derby and drawing with Wimbledon.

Spirit

When Liverpool thumped West Ham 5-1 to send the East Enders down, no-one gave the Gunners a prayer of winning by two.

They had not scored two goals at Anfield since 1974, when Alan Ball scored twice and Liam Brady once. They had lost their last seven First Division games here.

There were more omens in Liverpool's favour. John Aldridge and Ian Rush had never been on a losing side in partnership, while goalkeeper Bruce Grobbelaar had not been on a losing

side in 28 games this season, keeping 13 clean sheets.

It was stacked against Arsenal, but there was an amazing spirit within the camp. They actually believed they could pull it off.

Graham said before the game he was very optimistic. David Rocastle revealed that none of the players was frightened by the daunting task ahead of them.

Even without two of their best players, Brian Marwood and Paul Davis, Arsenal clinched their ninth championship in a remarkable performance.

They strode out with each player holding a bouquet which they presented to the fans.

The Gunners were determined not to leave Anfield empty-handed, while Liverpool were favourites to add the title to the FA Cup they had won at Wembley by overwhelming Everton in another exciting match.

Graham began the game sitting in the directors' box alongside his chairman Peter Hill-Wood and vice-chairman David Dein.

By the start of the second half he was down on the bench.

The Gunners might have taken an early goal

when a cross from Thomas was misjudged by Grobbelaar and Steve Bould's header was goalbound until Steve Nicol headed it over his own bar.

Although Bould was recalled as Graham gambled by reinstating his sweeper system, Arsenal were always ready to attack.

A breakthrough goal after 52 minutes, 13 seconds put the championship on a knife-edge.

Liverpool skipper Ronnie Whelan fouled Rocastle and Nigel Winterburn's free-kick was headed into the corner by Alan Smith.

Booked

Liverpool fervently protested that Smith's 25th goal of the season — his 23rd in the League — should not have counted because referee David Hutchinson had raised his arm for an indirect free kick and the Liverpool camp were insistent that Smith had not got a touch.

Dalglish was on the touchline as both sets of players surrounded the referee in his consultations with the linesman. But the goal was given and suddenly Arsenal took total command.

Thomas stabbed a 74th minute chance created by Kevin Richardson straight at Grobbelaar from close range, and Arsenal's hopes seemed to falter.

Graham pulled off Paul Merson, bringing on Martin Hayes. A few minutes later he brought off Bould, substituting him with Perry Groves.

Richardson was booked for a foul on

Ray Houghton and Rocastle was shown the yellow card for dissent.

Houghton was put in the clear by Aldridge with just seven minutes to go, but blasted his shot over when he could have picked his spot.

As the minutes ticked away, Arsenal were so much on the offensive that John Barnes was forced to play centre-half, heading out a Groves cross as Liverpool were pinned back in their own half.

Liverpool broke and Beardsley and Aldridge faced just one defender. But Aldridge, with 29 goals this season, lacked the technique to control the ball as it bounced away from him.

As the game spilled into injury time Barnes robbed Arsenal skipper Tony Adams, setting off on a dribble which never came off. Lukic threw the ball out to Lee Dixon, his long ball was knocked on by Smith and there was Thomas in the clear.

Thomas had so much

space and time it seemed to take an eternity before he struck the championship-deciding shot past a helpless Grobbelaar.

Aldridge dropped to his knees, Barnes lay on his back and David O'Leary was in tears. The Gunners' longest-serving player had finally tasted championship success.

The Barclays title comes to London and no one in the 41,718 crowd or the millions watching at home can begrudge the Gunners their greatest triumph.

CHAMPION! Alan Smith (left) and Michael Thomas get their reward.

MIRACLE

● From Back Page

match because although it was hard it was never a dirty game.

"Thomas got our vital goal and he deserves an awful lot of credit. He has grown up in the latter part of the season not only as a player but also as a man."

Thomas said: "I can't put it into words exactly how I feel. It is just so wonderful for everybody that we did it in style.

"It is tremendous to score a goal like th

players were weeping tears of j

183

–LEGENDS–

David O'Leary

A product of Arsenal's youth system, O'Leary made his debut just three months after his 17th birthday in 1975. His first task was to help steer an ageing side clear of relegation. The Republic of Ireland international was an imperious centre-half, full of grace both in his use of the ball and his demeanour on the pitch. He oozed calmness too, rarely belting the ball clear when there was an opportunity to create from the back, and gained the nickname "Spider" for his ability to cover ground and intercept passes.

While others sought pastures new at the start of the 1980s, O'Leary remained at Highbury, building on his reputation to become one of the game's most complete defenders. But it took the arrival of George Graham before O'Leary's talents were rewarded with medals. The first was the Littlewoods Cup in 1987, though this proved to be the last season in which he would command a regular place in the side.

An ankle injury sidelined him for much of the following campaign and his involvement in the 1989 title success was sporadic. He won another League Championship medal in 1991 before his swansong season in 1993 brought more domestic silverware. He left that summer for Leeds, as Arsenal's all-time record appearance holder.

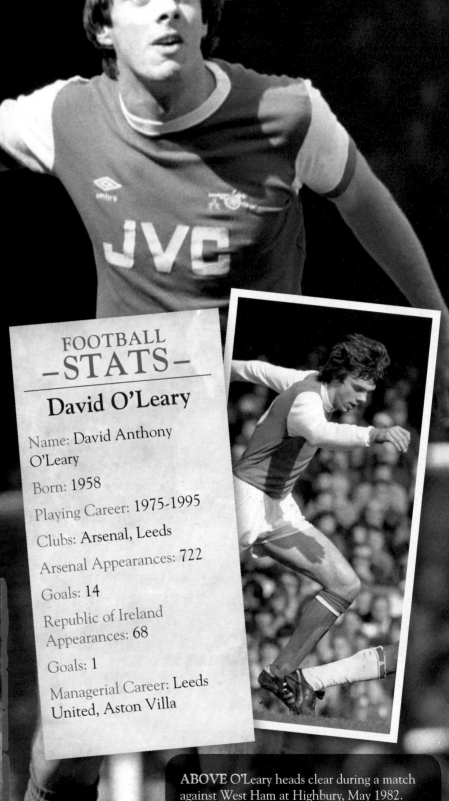

FOOTBALL –STATS–

David O'Leary

Name: David Anthony O'Leary

Born: 1958

Playing Career: 1975-1995

Clubs: Arsenal, Leeds

Arsenal Appearances: 722

Goals: 14

Republic of Ireland Appearances: 68

Goals: 1

Managerial Career: Leeds United, Aston Villa

ABOVE O'Leary heads clear during a match against West Ham at Highbury, May 1982.

LEFT With girlfriend Joy Lewis, May 1979.

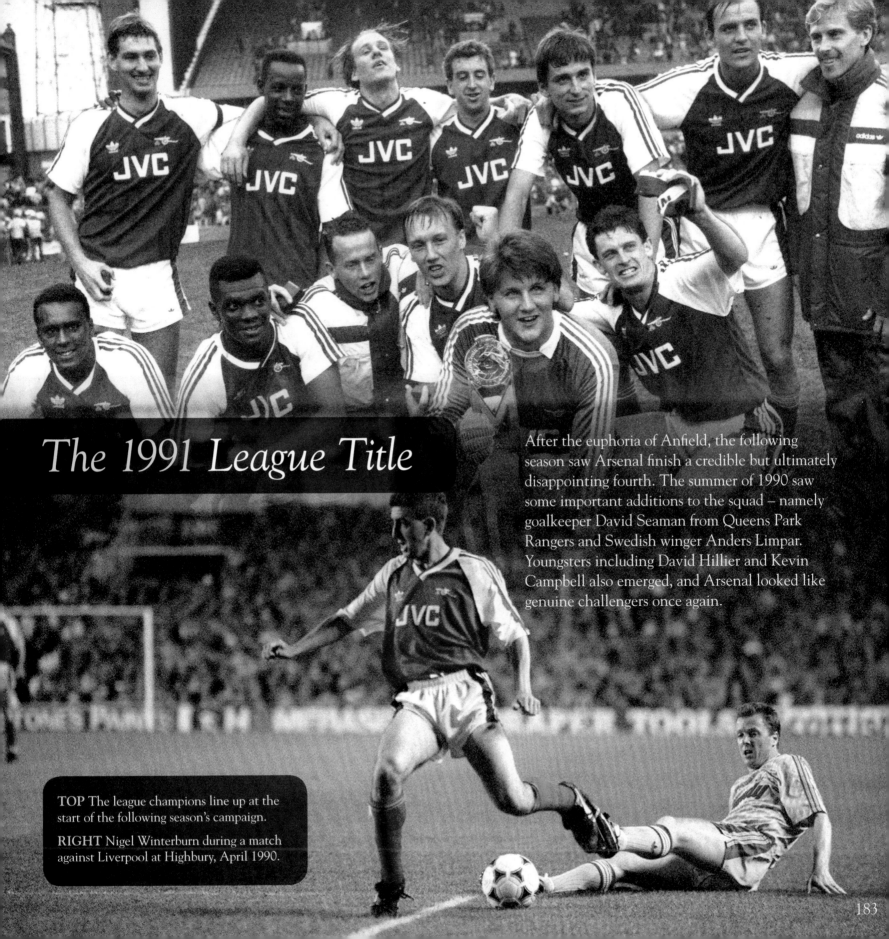

The 1991 League Title

After the euphoria of Anfield, the following season saw Arsenal finish a credible but ultimately disappointing fourth. The summer of 1990 saw some important additions to the squad – namely goalkeeper David Seaman from Queens Park Rangers and Swedish winger Anders Limpar. Youngsters including David Hillier and Kevin Campbell also emerged, and Arsenal looked like genuine challengers once again.

TOP The league champions line up at the start of the following season's campaign.

RIGHT Nigel Winterburn during a match against Liverpool at Highbury, April 1990.

ABOVE A snow-bound Highbury, 1991.

OPPOSITE RIGHT A policeman checking a fan's jacket outside the stadium, March 1990.

OPPOSITE FAR RIGHT An entrance to Highbury's West Stand, 1990.

ARSENAL FOOTBALL CLUB

ARSENAL SUPPORTERS ONLY

GROUND ADMISSION £4.00

WEST STAND UPPER TIER

> "At Arsenal we never started any brawls – we just finished them."
>
> David Rocastle

ABOVE Players come to blows during Arsenal's 1-0 victory against Manchester United at Old Trafford, October 1990. The protagonists in the 21-man brawl (only David Seaman did not get involved) were Nigel Winterburn and Brian McClair, who had previously clashed at Highbury in 1988 when Winterburn goaded McClair for missing a penalty.

OPPOSITE Despite the club acting quickly by fining boss George Graham and a number of players, Arsenal still felt the full force of the Football Association's wrath. They were docked two points, while United received a slightly more lenient punishment. The reason given for the discrepancy was Arsenal's "previous" – namely a similar brawl against Norwich City at Highbury in 1990.

MIRROR SPORT

VERDICT
ON THE BRAWL CLUBS
WHO SHAMED SOCCER

ARSENAL 2 UNITED 1

 Points docked

 £50,000 fines

GUILTY

TITLE-CHASING Arsenal were sensation-ally deducted two League points and fined £50,000 last night.

Manchester United were also fined £50,000 and docked one point in an unprecedented FA backlash following last month's infamous Battle of Old Trafford.

Managers George Graham and Alex Ferguson looked shell-shocked after the disciplinary crack-down on the 21-man brawl at Old Trafford on October 20 which scandalised soccer.

Arsenal are now a massive eight points adrift of Liverpool and shattered Highbury de-fender David O'Leary said: "The champagne will be out at Anfield to-night. The FA have as good as handed them the League title.

Sad

"Without disparaging anybody else, we are the team who could really have challenged Liver-pool this season. It's very sad – we didn't think they would take points off us."

And Manchester United defender Dennis Irwin, one of the men originally involved in the Old Trafford fracas, added: "I am very sur-prised. Both clubs were expecting fines but to take points away seems a bit silly.

"It all happened in the heat of the moment and we just wanted to forget about it. The referee didn't send anybody off and the rest of the game was OK. There were no problems with us and the Arsenal players.

"Every point counts and you need as many as you can get when you're chasing Liver-

By FRANK WIECHULA

pool. This certainly helps them."

A five-man FA com-mission meeting in Lon-don took 3½ hours to throw the book at the two teams, who were also censured and warned as to their fu-ture conduct.

But it was the com-mission's punishment of Arsenal and the effect on their title bid which has sent shock waves through soccer.

A giant hole has been blown in Arsenal's championship challenge, with leaders Liverpool now holding an enor-mous advantage over their biggest rivals.

Retiring PFA chair-man Garth Crooks said: "It's like giving Ni-jinsky in full flight an extra furlong – and you can't do that to Liverpool."

Arsenal boss George Graham and chairman

◀ Turn to Page 30

FLASHPOINT

THIS was the moment of madness when Arsenal and Manchester United were involved in a 21-man brawl at Old Trafford. But the FA made them pay the ultimate penalty yesterday.

Published by Mirror Group Newspapers (1986) Ltd, at 33 Holborn, London EC1P 1DQ (071-353 0246) and printed by Mirror Colour Print Ltd. Registered as a newspaper at the Post Office. Serial No. 27,234. © The Daily Mirror Newspapers, Ltd. 1990. Tuesday, November

–LEGENDS–

David Rocastle

South London-born Rocastle came through the ranks at Highbury in the mid-1980s bringing flair to Arsenal's midfield with a combination of pace, poise and vision. He won the Supporters' Player of the Year award in 1986 and picked up his first major honour the following campaign with the Littlewoods Cup. Rocastle's growth continued apace and over the next two seasons he didn't miss a league game, culminating with the title success of 1989. He ended that dramatic season as the Barclays Young Eagle of the Year. He also quickly stamped his mark on the international scene, gaining 10 England caps before his 23rd birthday.

Having played a major part in the title triumph of 1991, the following season saw him flourish in a new central position as Arsenal finished the campaign with some stunning football – though they would fail to reclaim the title. Rocastle looked set to assume his new role for years to come but, in the summer of 1992, he was surprisingly sold to Leeds. Such was his reluctance to leave, he was in floods of tears as he said goodbye to team-mates and club staff. Rocastle's career never scaled the same heights again, as injuries took their toll. He died of cancer in March 2001, aged just 33.

TOP Rocastle, a title-winner in 1989.

RIGHT Being restrained by the Southampton goalkeeper at Highbury, December 1986.

188

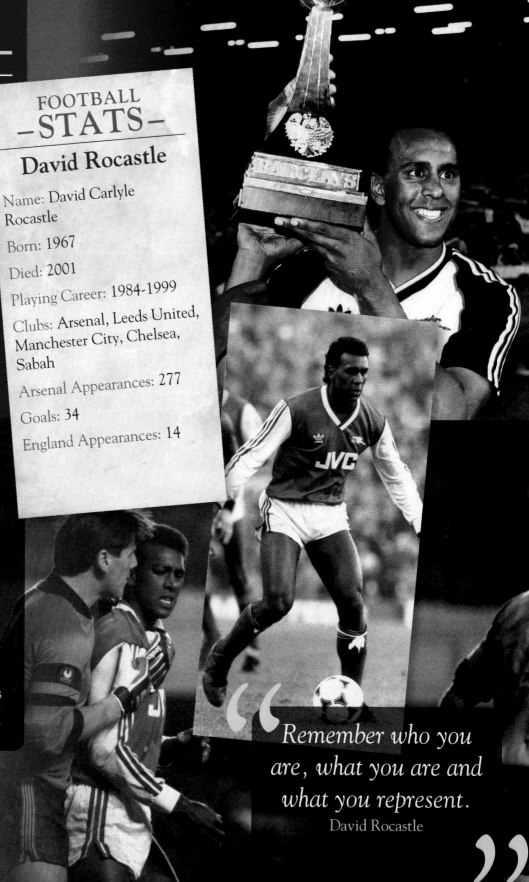

FOOTBALL –STATS–

David Rocastle

Name: David Carlyle Rocastle

Born: 1967

Died: 2001

Playing Career: 1984-1999

Clubs: Arsenal, Leeds United, Manchester City, Chelsea, Sabah

Arsenal Appearances: 277

Goals: 34

England Appearances: 14

"*Remember who you are, what you are and what you represent.*
David Rocastle"

In December 1990 Tony Adams was sentenced to four months in Chelmsford Prison for drink-driving offences. At the time, few were aware of his problems with alcoholism, which were only made public in later years when Adams set about transforming his life. It was a traumatic time for the captain, and for those close to him, including his team-mates.

The club stuck by him, continuing to pay his wages while he served his sentence (he was released after two months) and on the pitch Arsenal coped admirably in his absence – defender Andy Linighan proving an able deputy. Everyone within the club were determined they would still be in the hunt for the title when Adams returned to action.

GREAT TO BE BACK

TONY ADAMS couldn't contain his joy after his reserve team come-back at Highbury.

Next Wednesday he'll have more to shout about when he pulls on an England shirt again.

Picture: ARNOLD SLATER

England soccer ace Tony is caged for drink driving

> " *We shall win that title and we shall win it for Tony.*
> Paul Merson "

LEFT Paul Merson slots the ball past Bruce Grobbelaar for Arsenal's winner against Liverpool at Anfield, March 1991. It was a victory that put Arsenal in the title driving seat.

BELOW LEFT Merson and midfielder David Hillier celebrate the Anfield goal.

OPPOSITE Paul Davis (number 8) on his knees after scoring with a spectacular overhead kick in a 5-0 victory over Aston Villa at Highbury, April 1991.

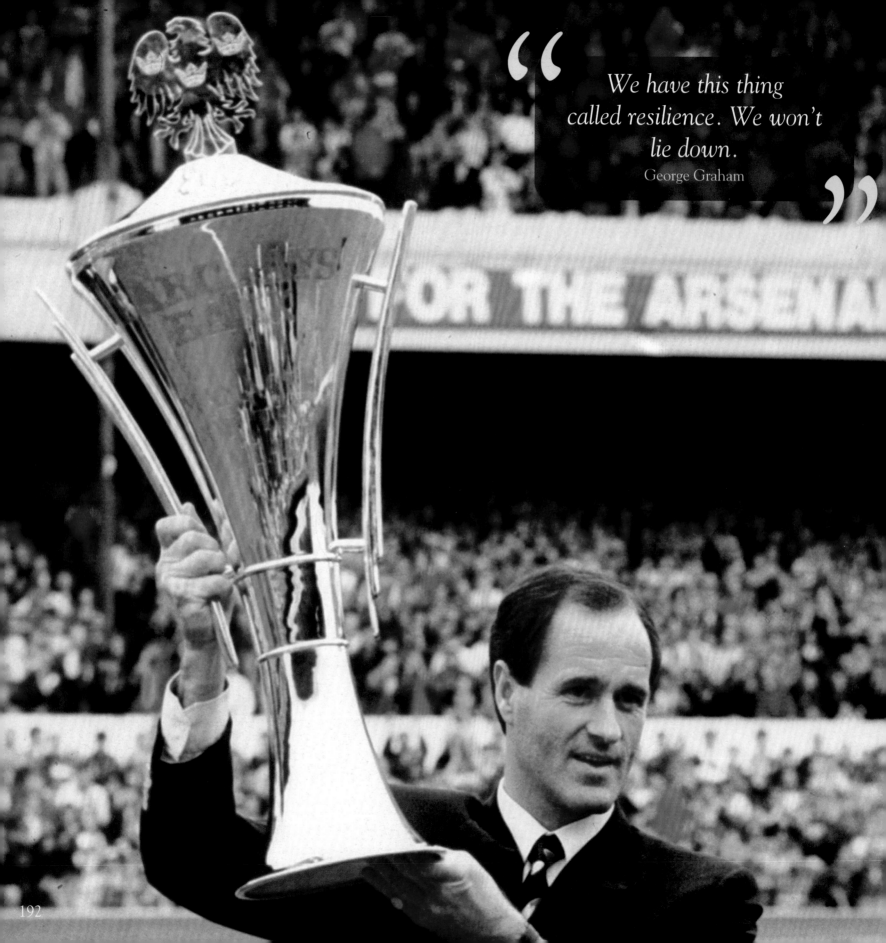

> "We have this thing called resilience. We won't lie down."
>
> George Graham

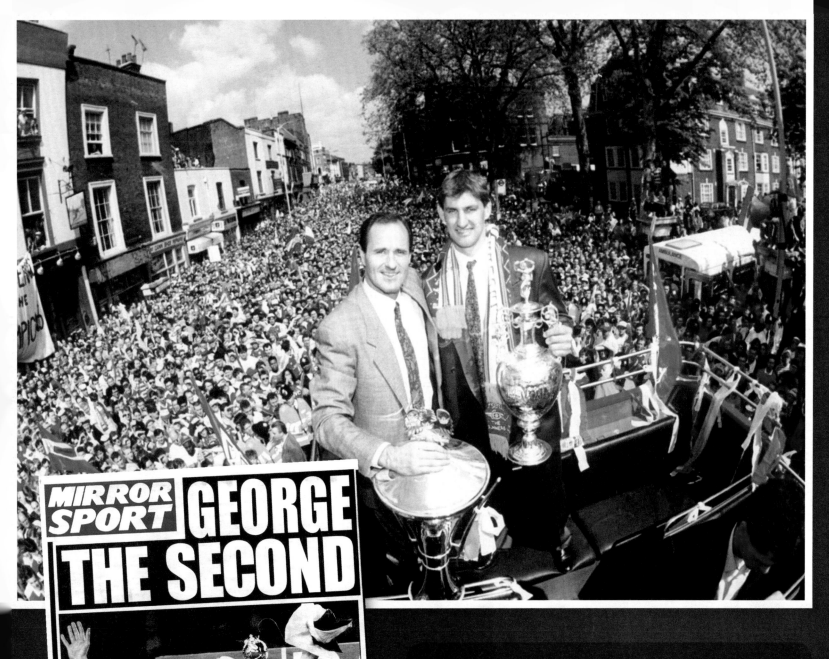

MIRROR SPORT **GEORGE THE SECOND**

ABOVE Graham and Tony Adams during the traditional open-top bus parade around Islington.

LEFT A *Daily Mirror* cutting shows David O'Leary, Steve Bould and Tony Adams celebrating Arsenal's 1991 League Championship triumph with the Barclays trophy after a 3-1 victory over Manchester United at Highbury. Arsenal won the title, losing just one league game all season.

OPPOSITE George Graham receives the Barclays Manager of the Year trophy after Arsenal's 6-1 victory over Coventry City in the final game of the season, May 1991.

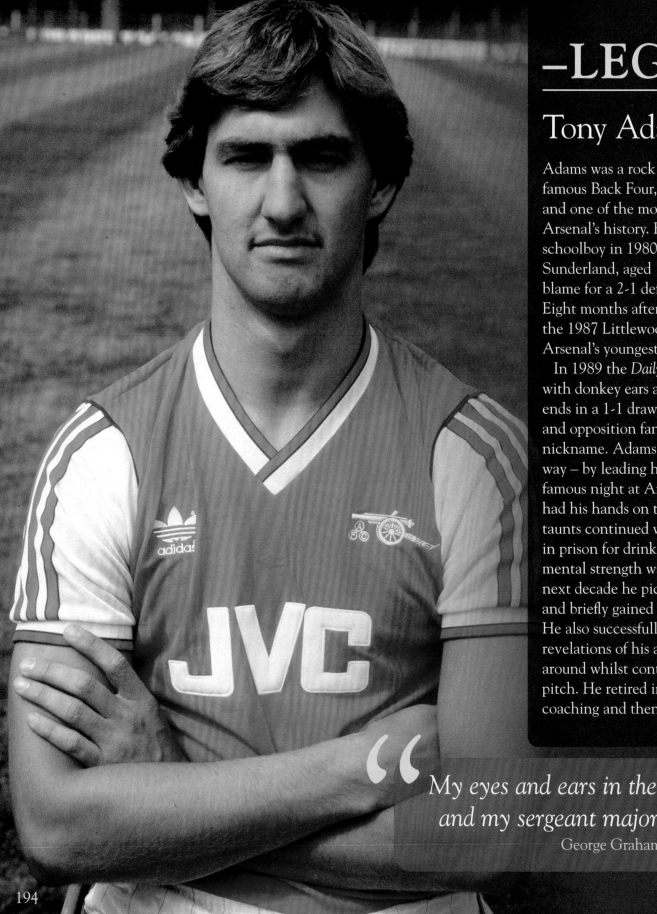

–LEGENDS–

Tony Adams

Adams was a rock at the heart of Arsenal's famous Back Four, the ultimate one-club man, and one of the most inspirational players in Arsenal's history. He signed for the club as a schoolboy in 1980, making his debut against Sunderland, aged 17. He was partly held to blame for a 2-1 defeat, but soon found his feet. Eight months after winning his first medal at the 1987 Littlewoods Cup final, he became Arsenal's youngest ever skipper aged 21.

In 1989 the *Daily Mirror* depicted him with donkey ears after he scored at both ends in a 1-1 draw at Manchester United, and opposition fans soon latched on to the nickname. Adams responded in the best way – by leading his team to the title on that famous night at Anfield. Two years later he had his hands on the same trophy, though the taunts continued when he spent two months in prison for drink-driving. But Adams's mental strength was unyielding. Over the next decade he picked up a host of silverware, and briefly gained the England captaincy. He also successfully came through the public revelations of his alcoholism to turn his life around whilst continuing to excel on the pitch. He retired in 2002 before going into coaching and then management.

> *My eyes and ears in the dressing room and my sergeant major on the pitch.*
> George Graham

FOOTBALL
–STATS–

Tony Adams

Name: Anthony Alexander Adams

Born: 1966

Playing Career: 1983-2002

Clubs: Arsenal

Arsenal Appearances: 669

Goals: 48

England Appearances: 66

Goals: 5

Managerial Career: Wycombe Wanderers, Portsmouth

TOP With England manager Bobby Robson, March 1988.

RIGHT Adams with the Young Player of the Month award, October 1986.

> " *Ian could be the most expensive substitute in history.*
> George Graham "

Ian Wright poses in his new club colours after signing for Arsenal from Crystal Palace for £2.5 million. He quickly brought a vibrancy to Highbury that had been missing since the departure of Charlie Nicolas.

BELOW Lee Dixon after his memorable own goal against Coventry at Highbury during a 2-1 defeat, when he contrived to lob David Seaman from 25 yards, September 1991. Even assistant manager Stewart Houston (far left) appears to be stifling a giggle in the dugout.

OPPOSITE TOP LEFT Alan Smith celebrates scoring against Austria Vienna at Highbury during a 6-1 victory in the European Cup, September 1991.

RIGHT The *Daily Mirror* highlights the financial implications of Arsenal's European Cup exit at the hands of Benfica, November 1991.

ABOVE Steve Watkins celebrates his winning goal in Wrexham's shock FA Cup victory over Arsenal, January 1992.

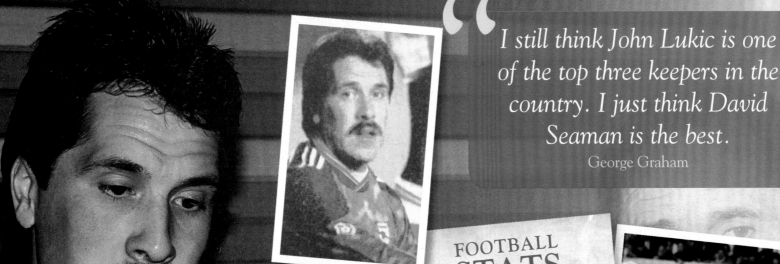

FOOTBALL
–STATS–

David Seaman

Name: David Andrew Seaman

Born: 1963

Playing Career: 1982-2004

Clubs: Peterborough United, Birmingham City, Queens Park Rangers, Arsenal, Manchester City

Arsenal Appearances: 564

England Appearances: 75

–LEGENDS–

David Seaman

Without George Graham's quest for perfection, David Seaman would have never arrived at Highbury. Arsenal already had a capable goalkeeper in John Lukic, but Graham wanted the best. Seaman moved from Queens Park Rangers in the Spring of 1990. At the time the fee of £1.3 million, a British record for a goalkeeper, was thought excessive by some – including sceptical Arsenal fans. In hindsight, it can be considered some of the best money Graham ever spent.

   Seaman's qualities were numerous. He had sharp reflexes, excellent positional sense, and an understated style that meant he would always forego the "Hollywood" save in favour of the simple but effective. His consistency became the cornerstone of an Arsenal back five which kept 23 clean sheets and conceded just 18 goals en route to the 1990/91 league title. The trophies continued to stack up at club level, whilst he established himself as England's Number One, eventually raising his profile to the status of national celebrity. After 564 appearances and eight major trophies, he left to join Manchester City in 2003.

–LEGENDS–

Ian Wright

Ian Wright was a bundle of energy, personality and goals. The volume and variety of his strikes marked him out as one of the greatest forwards of his generation, equally capable of a close-range tap-in, a 30-yard screamer, or an intricate dribble through a defence followed by a slide-rule finish. He was also a practical joker in the dressing room and king of the choreographed, theatrical goal celebration.

Wright's reputation as a prolific goalscorer had been established during his amateur days and he took this on to the professional stage, scoring 117 goals in six seasons for Crystal Palace. His move to Arsenal in September 1991 for a club record £2.5 million was only surprising because, on face value, the reigning title-holders didn't need a new striker. Wright started as he meant to go on, scoring a debut goal at Leicester followed by a hat-trick against Southampton. The following season his goals spearheaded Arsenal to an unprecedented domestic Cup Double.

Wright's only flaw was his discipline – he was often suspended and may as well have had his own parking space at FA headquarters. Whether this affected his international chances remains open to debate, but Graham Taylor's decision to leave him out of England's 1992 European Championship squad was bizarre given he had won the Golden Boot the previous campaign. Wright left Highbury in 1998 as the club's all-time record goalscorer, moving to West Ham before spells at Celtic and Burnley. He is now a television and radio presenter.

FOOTBALL –STATS–

Ian Wright

Name: Ian Edward Wright

Born: 1963

Playing Career: 1984-2000

Clubs: Greenwich Borough, Crystal Palace, Arsenal, West Ham, Celtic, Burnley

Arsenal Appearances: 288

Goals: 185

England Appearances: 33

Goals: 9

TOP LEFT Ian Wright celebrates with David Rocastle, Michael Thomas and Paul Davis after his debut goal against Leicester, September 1991.

TOP RIGHT Swedish winger Anders Limpar after scoring a 45-yard lobbed goal in a 4-0 victory over Liverpool at Highbury, April 1992.

RIGHT Wright takes the applause after one of his four goals during a 4-2 win over Everton at Highbury, December 1991. Anders Limpar created all four for Wright that day.

–LEGENDS–

George Graham

Numerous capable managers had dutifully served the club both on the pitch and in the dugout, but George Graham's success in both roles makes him unique in Arsenal's history. When Graham the free-scoring forward moved from Chelsea to Arsenal in September 1966, he picked up where he left off, topping Arsenal's scoring charts in his first two seasons. Despite this success, in early 1969 Bertie Mee moved Graham to a central midfield role. From his new position Graham helped Arsenal claim the Fairs Cup in 1970 and the League and FA Cup Double a season later, including a Man of the Match performance in the Cup final. However Alan Ball's arrival midway through the following season cast doubt on Graham's future, and in December 1972 he joined Manchester United.

Thirteen years later Graham returned to Highbury as manager, and instantly stamped his authoritative mark on the club. His office approach was in stark contrast to his playing days: the man they called "Stroller" for his laconic style was now a staunch disciplinarian who valued work ethic above all other qualities. In his first season in charge he lifted the Littlewoods Cup and in 1989 he became the first man to win the title with Arsenal as a player and a manager. Graham led Arsenal to another title in 1991, a domestic Cup Double in 1993 and the European Cup Winners' Cup in 1994 before his departure in 1995 amid "bung" allegations. He later managed Leeds and then, to every Arsenal fan's horror, Tottenham.

FOOTBALL
–STATS–

George Graham

Name: George Graham

Born: 1944

Playing Career: 1961-1978

Clubs: Aston Villa, Chelsea, Arsenal, Manchester United, Portsmouth, Crystal Palace, California Surf

Arsenal Appearances: 38

Goals: 77

Scotland Appearances: 12

Goals: 3

Managerial Career: Millwall, Arsenal, Leeds United, Tottenham Hotspur

David Dein, **a key figure in the** controversial **Bond Scheme.**

ARSENAL SENSATION

HIGH-BOO-RY

Fans turn on George  **Fans stage bond demo**

GOODBYE NORTH BANK!

THE SHAPE OF THINGS TO COME!

AN artist's impression of the new North Bank stand at Highbury

Tucked away in the last match day programme of the 1990/91 season against Coventry City was an advertisement for a new season ticket scheme at Highbury. The promotion went largely unnoticed amid the title celebrations, but within a year the proposal had become a huge source of contention amongst fans.

In response to the Taylor Report on the Hillsborough tragedy that dictated all top division grounds in the country had to be converted into all-seater stadiums, Arsenal had decided to finance their own redevelopment with a controversial Bond Scheme. The North Bank terrace would be demolished and replaced by an all-singing, all-dancing, all-sitting 12,500-capacity stand.

At the forefront of the plans were directors David Dein and Danny Fizman, with the former bearing the brunt of supporters' rage. Fans mobilized and held a series of demonstrations to stop the board in their tracks, but it was all in vain. The famous old North Bank, which held so many cherished memories for Arsenal fans down the ages, would be razed to the ground at the end of the 1991/92 season. For many it meant more than the end of an era: it was a nail in the coffin of the club's heart and soul.

ABOVE Ian Wright takes a shot at goal during the final game of the 1991-92 season –
a 5-1 victory over Southampton. A Wright hat-trick meant he overtook Tottenham's
Gary Lineker as the league's top goalscorer for the season. The final whistle saw fans in
floods of tears as they said goodbye to their beloved North Bank. Many refused to leave
and staged a final sit-in protest before being removed by police.

The North Bank, Highbury 1913/1992.